www.EffortlessMath.com

... So Much More Online!

✓ FREE Math lessons

✓ More Math learning books!

✓ Mathematics Worksheets

✓ Online Math Tutors

Need a PDF version of this book?

Please visit www.EffortlessMath.com

ISEE Upper Level Math Study Guide 2022- 2023

Step-By-Step Guide to Preparing for the ISEE Upper Level Math Test

By

Reza Nazari

Copyright © 2021

Effortless Math Education Inc.

All inquiries should be addressed to:
info@effortlessMath.com
www.EffortlessMath.com

ISBN: 978-1-63719-037-1

Published by: **Effortless Math Education Inc.**

For Online Math Practice Visit www.EffortlessMath.com

Welcome to
ISEE Upper Level Math
2022

Thank you for choosing Effortless Math for your ISEE Upper Level Math test preparation and congratulations on making the decision to take the ISEE Upper Level test! It's a remarkable move you are taking, one that shouldn't be diminished in any capacity. That's why you need to use every tool possible to ensure you succeed on the test with the highest possible score, and this extensive study guide is one such tool.

This book will help you prepare for (and even ACE) the ISEE Upper Level test's math section. As test day draws nearer, effective preparation becomes increasingly more important. Thankfully, you have this comprehensive study guide to help you get ready for the test. With this guide, you can feel confident that you will be more than ready for the ISEE Upper Level Math test when the time comes.

First and foremost, it is important to note that this book is a study guide and not a textbook. It is best read from cover to cover. Every lesson of this "self-guided math book" was carefully developed to ensure that you are making the most effective use of your time while preparing for the test. This up-to-date guide reflects the 2022 test guidelines and will put you on the right track to hone your math skills, overcome exam anxiety, and boost your confidence, so that you can have your best to succeed on the ISEE Upper Level Math test.

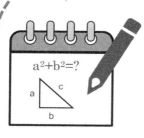

This study guide will:

- ☑ Explain the format of the ISEE Upper Level Math test.

- ☑ Describe specific test-taking strategies that you can use on the test.

- ☑ Provide ISEE Upper Level Math test-taking tips.

- ☑ Review all ISEE Upper Level Math concepts and topics you will be tested on.

- ☑ Help you identify the areas in which you need to concentrate your study time.

- ☑ Offer exercises that help you develop the basic math skills you will learn in each section.

- ☑ Give **2 realistic and full-length practice tests** (featuring new question types) with detailed answers to help you measure your exam readiness and build confidence.

This resource contains everything you will ever need to succeed on the ISEE Upper Level Math test. You'll get in-depth instructions on every math topic as well as tips and techniques on how to answer each question type. You'll also get plenty of practice questions to boost your test-taking confidence.

In addition, in the following pages you'll find:

➢ **How to Use This Book Effectively** – This section provides you with step-by-step instructions on how to get the most out of this comprehensive study guide.

➢ **How to study for the ISEE Upper Level Math Test** – A six-step study program has been developed to help you make the best use of this book and prepare for your ISEE Upper Level Math test. Here you'll find tips and strategies to guide your study program and help you understand ISEE Upper Level Math and how to ace the test.

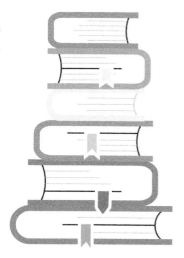

➤ **ISEE Upper Level Math Review** – Learn everything you need to know about the ISEE Upper Level Math test.

➤ **ISEE Upper Level Math Test-Taking Strategies** – Learn how to effectively put these recommended test-taking techniques into use for improving your ISEE Upper Level Math score.

➤ **Test Day Tips** – Review these tips to make sure you will do your best when the big day comes.

Effortless Math's ISEE Upper Level Online Center

Effortless Math Online ISEE Upper Level Center offers a complete study program, including the following:

✓ Step-by-step instructions on how to prepare for the ISEE Upper Level Math test

✓ Numerous ISEE Upper Level Math worksheets to help you measure your math skills

✓ Complete list of ISEE Upper Level Math formulas

✓ Video lessons for all ISEE Upper Level Math topics

✓ Full-length ISEE Upper Level Math practice tests

✓ And much more…

No Registration Required.

Visit effortlessmath.com/ISEE to find your online ISEE Upper Level Math resources.

How to Use This Book Effectively

Look no further when you need a study guide to improve your math skills to succeed on the math portion of the ISEE Upper Level test. Each chapter of this comprehensive guide to the ISEE Upper Level Math will provide you with the knowledge, tools, and understanding needed for every topic covered on the test.

It's imperative that you understand each topic before moving onto another one, as that's the way to guarantee your success. Each topic provides you with examples and a step-by-step guide of every concept to better understand the content that will be on the test. To get the best possible results from this book:

➢ **Begin studying long before your test date**. This provides you ample time to learn the different math concepts. The earlier you begin studying for the test, the sharper your skills will be. Do not procrastinate! Provide yourself with plenty of time to learn the concepts and feel comfortable that you understand them when your test date arrives.

➢ **Practice consistently**. Study ISEE Upper Level Math concepts at least 20 to 30 minutes a day. Remember, slow and steady wins the race, which can be applied to preparing for the ISEE Upper Level Math test. Instead of cramming to tackle everything at once, be patient and learn the math topics in short bursts.

➢ Whenever you get a math problem wrong, **mark it off, and review it later** to make sure you understand the concept.

➢ Start each session by **looking over the previous material.**

➢ Once you've reviewed the book's lessons, **take the practice test at the back of the book** to gauge your level of readiness. Then, review your results. Read detailed answers and solutions for each question you missed.

➢ **Take another practice test** to get an idea of how ready you are to take the actual exam. Taking the practice tests will give you the confidence you need on test day. Simulate the ISEE Upper Level testing environment by sitting in a quiet room free from distraction. Make sure to clock yourself with a timer.

How to Study for the ISEE Upper Level Math Test

Studying for the ISEE Upper Level Math test can be a really daunting and boring task. What's the best way to go about it? Is there a certain study method that works better than others? Well, studying for the ISEE Upper Level Math can be done effectively. The following six-step program has been designed to make preparing for the ISEE Upper Level Math test more efficient and less overwhelming.

Step **1** - Create a study plan
Step **2** - Choose your study resources
Step **3** - Review, Learn, Practice
Step **4** - Learn and practice test-taking strategies
Step **5** - Learn the ISEE Upper Level Test format and take practice tests
Step **6** - Analyze your performance

STEP 1: Create a Study Plan

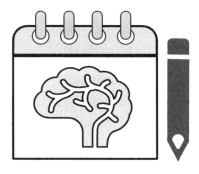

It's always easier to get things done when you have a plan. Creating a study plan for the ISEE Upper Level Math test can help you to stay on track with your studies. It's important to sit down and prepare a study plan with what works with your life, work, and any other obligations you may have. Devote enough time each day to studying. It's also a great idea to break down each section of the exam into blocks and study one concept at a time.

It's important to understand that there is no "right" way to create a study plan. Your study plan will be personalized based on your specific needs and learning style. Follow these guidelines to create an effective study plan for your ISEE Upper Level Math test:

★ **Analyze your learning style and study habits** – Everyone has a different learning style. It is essential to embrace your individuality and the unique way you learn. Think about what works and what doesn't work for you. Do you prefer ISEE Upper Level Math prep books or a combination of textbooks and video lessons? Does it work better for you if you study every night for thirty minutes or is it more effective to study in the morning before going to work?

★ **Evaluate your schedule** – Review your current schedule and find out how much time you can consistently devote to ISEE Upper Level Math study.

★ **Develop a schedule** – Now it's time to add your study schedule to your calendar like any other obligation. Schedule time for study, practice, and review. Plan out which topic you will study on which day to ensure that you're devoting enough time to each concept. Develop a study plan that is mindful, realistic, and flexible.

★ **Stick to your schedule** – A study plan is only effective when it is followed consistently. You should try to develop a study plan that you can follow for the length of your study program.

★ **Evaluate your study plan and adjust as needed** – Sometimes you need to adjust your plan when you have new commitments. Check in with yourself regularly to make sure that you're not falling behind in your study plan. Remember, the most important thing is sticking to your plan. Your study plan is all about helping you be more productive. If you find that your study plan is not as effective as you want, don't get discouraged. It's okay to make changes as you figure out what works best for you.

Step 2: Choose Your Study Resources

There are numerous textbooks and online resources available for the ISEE Upper Level Math test, and it may not be clear where to begin. Don't worry! This study guide provides everything you need to fully prepare for your ISEE Upper Level Math test. In addition to the book content, you can also use Effortless Math's online resources. (video lessons, worksheets, formulas, etc.) On each page, there is a 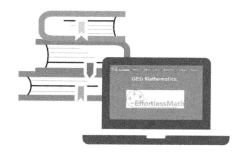 link (and a QR code) to an online webpage which provides a comprehensive review of the topic, step-by-step instruction, video tutorial, and numerous examples and exercises to help you fully understand the concept.

You can also visit EffortlessMath.com/ISEE to find your online ISEE Upper Level Math resources.

STEP 3: Review, Learn, Practice

This ISEE Upper Level Math study guide breaks down each subject into specific skills or content areas. For instance, the percent concept is separated into different topics–percent calculation, percent increase and decrease, percent problems, etc. Use this study guide and Effortless Math online ISEE Upper Level center to help you go over all key math concepts and topics on the ISEE Upper Level Math test.

As you read each topic, take notes or highlight the concepts you would like to go over again in the future. If you're unfamiliar with a topic or something is difficult for you, use the link (or the QR code) at the bottom of the page to find the webpage that provides more instruction about that topic. For each math topic, plenty of instructions, step-by-step guides, and examples are provided to ensure you get a good grasp of the material.

Quickly review the topics you do understand to get a brush-up of the material. Be sure to do the practice questions provided at the end of every chapter to measure your understanding of the concepts.

STEP 4: Learn and Practice Test-taking Strategies

In the following sections, you will find important test-taking strategies and tips that can help you earn extra points. You'll learn how to think strategically and when to guess if you don't know the answer to a question. Using ISEE Upper Level Math test-taking strategies and tips can help you raise your score and do well on the test. Apply test taking strategies on the practice tests to help you boost your confidence.

STEP 5: Learn the ISEE Upper Level Test Format and Take Practice Tests

The *ISEE Upper Level Test Review* section provides information about the structure of the ISEE Upper Level test. Read this section to learn more about the ISEE Upper Level test structure, different test sections, the number of questions in each section, and the section time limits. When you have a prior understanding of the test format and different types of ISEE Upper Level Math questions, you'll feel more confident when you take the actual exam.

Once you have read through the instructions and lessons and feel like you are ready to go – take advantage of both of the full-length ISEE Upper Level Math practice tests available in this study guide. Use the practice tests to sharpen your skills and build confidence.

The ISEE Upper Level Math practice tests offered at the end of the book are formatted similarly to the actual ISEE Upper Level Math test. When you take each practice test, try to simulate actual testing conditions. To take the practice tests, sit in a quiet space, time yourself, and work through as many of the questions as time allows. The practice tests are followed by detailed answer explanations to help you find your weak areas, learn from your mistakes, and raise your ISEE Upper Level Math score.

STEP 6: Analyze Your Performance

After taking the practice tests, look over the answer keys and explanations to learn which questions you answered correctly and which you did not. Never be discouraged if you make a few mistakes. See them as a learning opportunity. This will highlight your strengths and weaknesses.

You can use the results to determine if you need additional practice or if you are ready to take the actual ISEE Upper Level Math test.

Looking for more?

Visit <u>effortlessmath.com/ISEE</u> to find hundreds of ISEE Upper Level Math worksheets, video tutorials, practice tests, ISEE Upper Level Math formulas, and much more.

Or scan this QR code.

No Registration Required.

ISEE Upper Level Test Review

The Independent School Entrance Exam (ISEE) is a standardized test developed by the Educational Records Bureau for its member schools as part of their admission process.

There are currently four Levels of the ISEE:

- ✓ Primary Level (entering Grades 2 - 4)
- ✓ Lower Level (entering Grades 5 and 6)
- ✓ Middle Level (entering Grades 7 and 8)
- ✓ Upper Level (entering Grades 9 - 12)

There are five sections on the ISEE Upper Level Test:

- ○ Verbal Reasoning
- ○ Quantitative Reasoning
- ○ Reading Comprehension
- ○ Mathematics Achievement
- ○ and a 30-minute essay

ISEE Upper Level tests use a multiple-choice format and contain two Mathematics sections:

Quantitative Reasoning

There are 37 questions in the Quantitative Reasoning section and students have 35 minutes to answer the questions. This section contains word problems and quantitative comparisons. The word problems require either no calculation or simple calculation. The quantitative comparison items present two quantities, (A) and (B), and the student needs to select one of the following four answer choices:

(A) The quantity in Column A is greater.

(B) The quantity in Column B is greater.

(C) The two quantities are equal.

(D) The relationship cannot be determined from the information given.

Mathematics Achievement

There are 47 questions in the Mathematics Achievement section and students have 40 minutes to answer the questions. Mathematics Achievement measures students' knowledge of Mathematics requiring one or more steps in calculating the answer.

ISEE Upper Level Math Test-Taking Strategies

Here are some test-taking strategies that you can use to maximize your performance and results on the ISEE Upper Level Math test.

#1: USE THIS APPROACH TO ANSWER EVERY ISEE Upper Level MATH QUESTION

- Review the question to identify keywords and important information.

- Translate the keywords into math operations so you can solve the problem.

- Review the answer choices. What are the differences between answer choices?

- Draw or label a diagram if needed.

- Try to find patterns.

- Find the right method to answer the question. Use straightforward math, plug in numbers, or test the answer choices (backsolving).

- Double-check your work.

#2: USE EDUCATED GUESSING

This approach is applicable to the problems you understand to some degree but cannot solve using straightforward math. In such cases, try to filter out as many answer choices as possible before picking an answer. In cases where you don't have a clue about what a certain problem entails, don't waste any time trying to eliminate answer choices. Just choose one randomly before moving onto the next question.

As you can ascertain, direct solutions are the most optimal approach. Carefully read through the question, determine what the solution is using the math you have learned before, then coordinate the answer with one of the choices available to you. Are you stumped? Make your best guess, then move on.

Don't leave any fields empty! Even if you're unable to work out a problem, strive to answer it. Take a guess if you have to. You will not lose points by getting an answer wrong, though you may gain a point by getting it correct!

#3 : BALLPARK

A ballpark answer is a rough approximation. When we become overwhelmed by calculations and figures, we end up making silly mistakes. A decimal that is moved by one unit can change an answer from right to wrong, regardless of the number of steps that you went through to get it. That's where ballparking can play a big part.

If you think you know what the correct answer may be (even if it's just a ballpark answer), you'll usually have the ability to eliminate a couple of choices. While answer choices are usually based on the average student error and/or values that are closely tied, you will still be able to weed out choices that are way far afield. Try to find answers that aren't in the proverbial ballpark when you're looking for a wrong answer on a multiple-choice question. This is an optimal approach to eliminating answers to a problem.

#4 : BACKSOLVING

A majority of questions on the ISEE Upper Level Math test will be in multiple-choice format. Many test-takers prefer multiple-choice questions, as at least the answer is right there. You'll typically have four answers to pick from. You simply need to figure out which one is correct. Usually, the best way to go about doing so is "backsolving."

As mentioned earlier, direct solutions are the most optimal approach to answering a question. Carefully read through a problem, calculate a solution, then correspond the answer with one of the choices displayed in front of you. If you can't calculate a solution, your next best approach involves "backsolving."

When backsolving a problem, contrast one of your answer options against the problem you are asked, then see which of them is most relevant. More often than not, answer choices are listed in ascending or descending order. In such cases, try out the choices B or C. If it's not correct, you can go either down or up from there.

#5 : PLUGGING IN NUMBERS

"Plugging in numbers" is a strategy that can be applied to a wide range of different math problems on the ISEE Upper Level Math test. This approach is typically used to simplify a challenging question so that it is more understandable. By using the strategy carefully, you can find the answer without too much trouble.

The concept is fairly straightforward—replace unknown variables in a problem with certain values. When selecting a number, consider the following:

- Choose a number that's basic (just not too basic). Generally, you should avoid choosing 1 (or even 0). A decent choice is 2.

- Try not to choose a number that is displayed in the problem.

- Make sure you keep your numbers different if you need to choose at least two of them.

- More often than not, choosing numbers merely lets you filter out some of your answer choices. As such, don't just go with the first choice that gives you the right answer.

- If several answers seem correct, then you'll need to choose another value and try again. This time, though, you'll just need to check choices that haven't been eliminated yet.

- If your question contains fractions, then a potential right answer may involve either an LCD (least common denominator) or an LCD multiple.

- 100 is the number you should choose when you are dealing with problems involving percentages.

ISEE Upper Level Math – Test Day Tips

After practicing and reviewing all the math concepts you've been taught, and taking some ISEE Upper Level mathematics practice tests, you'll be prepared for test day. Consider the following tips to be extra-ready come test time.

Before Your Test

What to do the night before:

- **Relax!** One day before your test, study lightly or skip studying altogether. You shouldn't attempt to learn something new, either. There are plenty of reasons why studying the evening before a big test can work against you. Put it this way–a marathoner wouldn't go out for a sprint before the day of a big race. Mental marathoners–such as yourself–should not study for any more than one hour 24 hours before a ISEE Upper Level test. That's because your brain requires some rest to be at its best. The night before your exam, spend some time with family or friends, or read a book.

- **Avoid bright screens** - You'll have to get some good shuteye the night before your test. Bright screens (such as the ones coming from your laptop, TV, or mobile device) should be avoided altogether. Staring at such a screen will keep your brain up, making it hard to drift asleep at a reasonable hour.

- **Make sure your dinner is healthy** - The meal that you have for dinner should be nutritious. Be sure to drink plenty of water as well. Load up on your complex carbohydrates, much like a marathon runner would do. Pasta, rice, and potatoes are ideal options here, as are vegetables and protein sources.

- **Get your bag ready for test day** - The night prior to your test, pack your bag with your stationery, admissions pass, ID, and any other gear that you need. Keep the bag right by your front door.

- **Make plans to reach the testing site** - Before going to sleep, ensure that you understand precisely how you will arrive at the site of the test. If parking is something you'll have to find first, plan for it. If you're dependent on public transit, then review the schedule. You should also make sure that the train/bus/subway/streetcar you use will be running. Find out about road closures

as well. If a parent or friend is accompanying you, ensure that they understand what steps they have to take as well.

The Day of the Test

- **Get up reasonably early, but not too early.**

- **Have breakfast** - Breakfast improves your concentration, memory, and mood. As such, make sure the breakfast that you eat in the morning is healthy. The last thing you want to be is distracted by a grumbling tummy. If it's not your own stomach making those noises, another test taker close to you might be instead. Prevent discomfort or embarrassment by consuming a healthy breakfast. Bring a snack with you if you think you'll need it.

- **Follow your daily routine** - Do you watch Good Morning America each morning while getting ready for the day? Don't break your usual habits on the day of the test. Likewise, if coffee isn't something you drink in the morning, then don't take up the habit hours before your test. Routine consistency lets you concentrate on the main objective—doing the best you can on your test.

- **Wear layers** - Dress yourself up in comfortable layers. You should be ready for any kind of internal temperature. If it gets too warm during the test, take a layer off.

- **Get there on time** - The last thing you want to do is get to the test site late. Rather, you should be there 45 minutes prior to the start of the test. Upon your arrival, try not to hang out with anybody who is nervous. Any anxious energy they exhibit shouldn't influence you.

- **Leave the books at home** - No books should be brought to the test site. If you start developing anxiety before the test, books could encourage you to do some last-minute studying, which will only hinder you. Keep the books far away—better yet, leave them at home.

- **Make your voice heard** - If something is off, speak to a proctor. If medical attention is needed or if you'll require anything, consult the proctor prior to the start of the test. Any doubts you have should be clarified. You should be entering the test site with a state of mind that is completely clear.

■ **Have faith in yourself** - When you feel confident, you will be able to perform at your best. When you are waiting for the test to begin, envision yourself receiving an outstanding result. Try to see yourself as someone who knows all the answers, no matter what the questions are. A lot of athletes tend to use this technique–particularly before a big competition. Your expectations will be reflected by your performance.

During your test

■ **Be calm and breathe deeply** - You need to relax before the test, and some deep breathing will go a long way to help you do that. Be confident and calm. You got this. Everybody feels a little stressed out just before an evaluation of any kind is set to begin. Learn some effective breathing exercises. Spend a minute meditating before the test starts. Filter out any negative thoughts you have. Exhibit confidence when having such thoughts.

■ **Concentrate on the test** - Refrain from comparing yourself to anyone else. You shouldn't be distracted by the people near you or random noise. Concentrate exclusively on the test. If you find yourself irritated by surrounding noises, earplugs can be used to block sounds off close to you. Don't forget–the test is going to last several hours if you're taking more than one subject of the test. Some of that time will be dedicated to brief sections. Concentrate on the specific section you are working on during a particular moment. Do not let your mind wander off to upcoming or previous sections.

■ **Skip challenging questions** - Optimize your time when taking the test. Lingering on a single question for too long will work against you. If you don't know what the answer is to a certain question, use your best guess, and mark the question so you can review it later on. There is no need to spend time attempting to solve something you aren't sure about. That time would be better served handling the questions you can actually answer well. You will not be penalized for getting the wrong answer on a test like this.

- **Try to answer each question individually** - Focus only on the question you are working on. Use one of the test-taking strategies to solve the problem. If you aren't able to come up with an answer, don't get frustrated. Simply skip that question, then move onto the next one.

- **Don't forget to breathe!** Whenever you notice your mind wandering, your stress levels boosting, or frustration brewing, take a thirty-second break. Shut your eyes, drop your pencil, breathe deeply, and let your shoulders relax. You will end up being more productive when you allow yourself to relax for a moment.

- **Review your answer.** If you still have time at the end of the test, don't waste it. Go back and check over your answers. It is worth going through the test from start to finish to ensure that you didn't make a sloppy mistake somewhere.

- **Optimize your breaks** - When break time comes, use the restroom, have a snack, and reactivate your energy for the subsequent section. Doing some stretches can help stimulate your blood flow.

After your test

- **Take it easy** - You will need to set some time aside to relax and decompress once the test has concluded. There is no need to stress yourself out about what you could've said, or what you may have done wrong. At this point, there's nothing you can do about it. Your energy and time would be better spent on something that will bring you happiness for the remainder of your day.

- **Redoing the test** - Did you pass the test? Congratulations! Your hard work paid off! Passing this test means that you are now as knowledgeable as somebody who has graduated high school.

  If you have failed your test, though, don't worry! The test can be retaken. In such cases, you will need to follow the retake policy established by your state. You also need to re-register to take the exam again.

Contents

Topic	**Simplifying Fractions**
Notes	✓ Evenly divide both the top and bottom of the fraction by 2, 3, 5, 7, ... etc. ✓ Continue until you can't go any further.
Example	***Simplify*** $\frac{36}{48}$ To simplify $\frac{36}{48}$, find a number that both 36 and 48 are divisible by. Both are divisible by 12. Then: $\frac{36}{48} = \frac{36 \div 12}{48 \div 12} = \frac{3}{4}$

Your Turn!	1) $\frac{3}{15} =$	2) $\frac{11}{55} =$
	3) $\frac{12}{48} =$	4) $\frac{11}{99} =$
	5) $\frac{15}{75} =$	6) $\frac{25}{100} =$
	7) $\frac{16}{72} =$	8) $\frac{32}{96} =$
	9) $\frac{15}{65} =$	10) $\frac{48}{92} =$

Find more at

bit.ly/3nOGNko

Topic	Simplifying Fractions – Answers
Notes	✓ Evenly divide both the top and bottom of the fraction by $2, 3, 5, 7, \dots$ etc. ✓ Continue until you can't go any further.
Example	*Simplify* $\frac{36}{48}$ To simplify $\frac{36}{48}$, find a number that both 36 and 48 are divisible by. Both are divisible by 12. Then: $\frac{36}{48} = \frac{36 \div 12}{48 \div 12} = \frac{3}{4}$

Your Turn!	1) $\frac{3}{15} = \frac{1}{5}$	2) $\frac{11}{55} = \frac{1}{5}$
	3) $\frac{12}{48} = \frac{1}{4}$	4) $\frac{11}{99} = \frac{1}{9}$
	5) $\frac{15}{75} = \frac{1}{5}$	6) $\frac{25}{100} = \frac{1}{4}$
	7) $\frac{16}{72} = \frac{2}{9}$	8) $\frac{32}{96} = \frac{1}{3}$
Find more at bit.ly/3nOGNko	9) $\frac{15}{65} = \frac{3}{13}$	10) $\frac{48}{92} = \frac{12}{23}$

Topic	**Adding and Subtracting Fractions**
Notes	✓ For "like" fractions (fractions with the same denominator), add or subtract the numerators and write the answer over the common denominator. ✓ Find equivalent fractions with the same denominator before you can add or subtract fractions with different denominators. ✓ Adding and Subtracting with the same denominator: $$\frac{a}{b}+\frac{c}{b}=\frac{a+c}{b}\ ,\ \frac{a}{b}-\frac{c}{b}=\frac{a-c}{b}$$ ✓ Adding and Subtracting fractions with different denominators: $$\frac{a}{b}+\frac{c}{d}=\frac{ad+bc}{bd}\ ,\ \frac{a}{b}-\frac{c}{d}=\frac{ad-bc}{bd}$$
Example	***Find the sum.*** $\frac{3}{5}+\frac{2}{3}=\frac{(3)3+(5)(2)}{5\times3}=\frac{19}{15}$ ***Subtract.*** $\frac{4}{7}-\frac{3}{7}=\frac{1}{7}$
Your Turn!	1) $\frac{2}{3}+\frac{1}{5}=$ 2) $\frac{8}{7}-\frac{3}{5}=$
	3) $\frac{4}{9}+\frac{5}{8}=$ 4) $\frac{5}{8}-\frac{2}{5}=$
	5) $\frac{2}{5}+\frac{1}{6}=$ 6) $\frac{2}{3}-\frac{1}{4}=$
Find more at bit.ly/3nKet2X	7) $\frac{8}{9}+\frac{5}{7}=$ 8) $\frac{6}{7}-\frac{5}{9}=$

Topic	Adding and Subtracting Fractions - Answers
Notes	✓ For "like" fractions (fractions with the same denominator), add or subtract the numerators and write the answer over the common denominator. ✓ Find equivalent fractions with the same denominator before you can add or subtract fractions with different denominators. ✓ Adding and Subtracting with the same denominator: $$\frac{a}{b} + \frac{c}{b} = \frac{a+c}{b}, \quad \frac{a}{b} - \frac{c}{b} = \frac{a-c}{b}$$ ✓ Adding and Subtracting fractions with different denominators: $$\frac{a}{b} + \frac{c}{d} = \frac{ad+bc}{bd}, \frac{a}{b} - \frac{c}{d} = \frac{ad-bc}{bd}$$
Example	*Find the sum.* $\frac{3}{5} + \frac{2}{3} = \frac{(3)3+(5)(2)}{5\times 3} = \frac{19}{15}$ *Subtract.* $\frac{4}{7} - \frac{3}{7} = \frac{1}{7}$

Your Turn!

1) $\frac{2}{3} + \frac{1}{5} = \frac{13}{15}$ 2) $\frac{8}{7} - \frac{3}{5} = \frac{19}{35}$

3) $\frac{4}{9} + \frac{5}{8} = \frac{77}{72}$ 4) $\frac{5}{8} - \frac{2}{5} = \frac{9}{40}$

5) $\frac{2}{5} + \frac{1}{6} = \frac{17}{30}$ 6) $\frac{2}{3} - \frac{1}{4} = \frac{5}{12}$

7) $\frac{8}{9} + \frac{5}{7} = \frac{101}{63}$ 8) $\frac{6}{7} - \frac{5}{9} = \frac{19}{63}$

Find more at

bit.ly/3nKet2X

Topic	Multiplying and Dividing Fractions
Notes	✓ Multiplying fractions: multiply the top numbers and multiply the bottom numbers. ✓ Dividing fractions: Keep, Change, Flip Keep first fraction, change division sign to multiplication, and flip the numerator and denominator of the second fraction. Then, solve!
Examples	**Multiply**. $\frac{2}{5} \times \frac{3}{4} =$ Multiply the top numbers and multiply the bottom numbers. $\frac{2}{5} \times \frac{3}{4} = \frac{2\times3}{5\times4} = \frac{6}{20}$, simplify: $\frac{6}{20} = \frac{6\div2}{20\div2} = \frac{3}{10}$ **Divide**. $\frac{2}{5} \div \frac{3}{4} =$ Keep first fraction, change division sign to multiplication, and flip the numerator and denominator of the second fraction. Then: $\frac{2}{5} \div \frac{3}{4} = \frac{2}{5} \times \frac{4}{3} = \frac{2\times4}{5\times3} = \frac{8}{15}$
Your Turn! **Find more at** bit.ly/3haSiQW	1) $\frac{3}{8} \times \frac{2}{5} =$ 2) $\frac{4}{9} \div \frac{3}{4} =$ 3) $\frac{2}{7} \times \frac{3}{5} =$ 4) $\frac{2}{5} \div \frac{7}{12} =$ 5) $\frac{1}{7} \times \frac{4}{9} =$ 6) $\frac{2}{9} \div \frac{3}{7} =$ 7) $\frac{4}{7} \times \frac{3}{8} =$ 8) $\frac{1}{6} \div \frac{3}{4} =$

Topic	**Multiplying and Dividing Fractions - Answers**
Notes	✓ Multiplying fractions: multiply the top numbers and multiply the bottom numbers. ✓ Dividing fractions: Keep, Change, Flip Keep first fraction, change division sign to multiplication, and flip the numerator and denominator of the second fraction. Then, solve!
Examples	*Multiply.* $\frac{2}{5} \times \frac{3}{4} =$ Multiply the top numbers and multiply the bottom numbers. $\frac{2}{5} \times \frac{3}{4} = \frac{2\times3}{5\times4} = \frac{6}{20}$, simplify: $\frac{6}{20} = \frac{6\div2}{20\div2} = \frac{3}{10}$ *Divide.* $\frac{2}{5} \div \frac{3}{4} =$ Keep first fraction, change division sign to multiplication, and flip the numerator and denominator of the second fraction. Then: $\frac{2}{5} \div \frac{3}{4} = \frac{2}{5} \times \frac{4}{3} = \frac{2\times4}{5\times3} = \frac{8}{15}$

Your Turn!		
	1) $\frac{3}{8} \times \frac{2}{5} = \frac{3}{20}$	2) $\frac{4}{9} \div \frac{3}{4} = \frac{16}{27}$
	3) $\frac{2}{7} \times \frac{3}{5} = \frac{6}{35}$	4) $\frac{2}{5} \div \frac{7}{12} = \frac{24}{35}$
	5) $\frac{1}{7} \times \frac{4}{9} = \frac{4}{63}$	6) $\frac{2}{9} \div \frac{3}{7} = \frac{14}{27}$
Find more at bit.ly/3haSiQW	7) $\frac{4}{7} \times \frac{3}{8} = \frac{3}{14}$	8) $\frac{1}{6} \div \frac{3}{4} = \frac{2}{9}$

Topic	**Adding Mixed Numbers**
Notes	Use the following steps for adding mixed numbers. ✓ Add whole numbers of the mixed numbers. ✓ Add the fractions of each mixed number. ✓ Find the Least Common Denominator (LCD) if necessary. ✓ Add whole numbers and fractions. ✓ Write your answer in lowest terms.
Example	***Add mixed numbers.*** $1\frac{1}{2} + 2\frac{2}{3} =$ Rewriting our equation with parts separated, $1 + \frac{1}{2} + 2 + \frac{2}{3}$ Add whole numbers: $1 + 2 = 3$ Add fractions: $\frac{1}{2} + \frac{2}{3} = \frac{3}{6} + \frac{4}{6} = \frac{7}{6} = 1\frac{1}{6}$, Now, combine the whole and fraction parts: $3 + 1 + \frac{1}{6} = 4\frac{1}{6}$

Your Turn!	1) $2\frac{1}{15} + 1\frac{2}{5} =$	2) $1\frac{3}{10} + 3\frac{1}{5} =$
	3) $1\frac{1}{10} + 2\frac{2}{5} =$	4) $2\frac{5}{6} + 2\frac{2}{9} =$
	5) $2\frac{2}{7} + 1\frac{2}{21} =$	6) $1\frac{3}{8} + 3\frac{2}{3} =$
Find more at bit.ly/2M4oAB	7) $1\frac{1}{6} + 4\frac{2}{7} =$	8) $2\frac{1}{6} + 1\frac{2}{5} =$

Topic	**Adding Mixed Numbers - Answers**
Notes	Use the following steps for adding mixed numbers. ✓ Add whole numbers of the mixed numbers. ✓ Add the fractions of each mixed number. ✓ Find the Least Common Denominator (LCD) if necessary. ✓ Add whole numbers and fractions. ✓ Write your answer in lowest terms.
Example	*Add mixed numbers.* $1\frac{1}{2} + 2\frac{2}{3} =$ Rewriting our equation with parts separated, $1 + \frac{1}{2} + 2 + \frac{2}{3}$ Add whole numbers: $1 + 2 = 3$ Add fractions: $\frac{1}{2} + \frac{2}{3} = \frac{3}{6} + \frac{4}{6} = \frac{7}{6} = 1\frac{1}{6}$ Now, combine the whole and fraction parts: $3 + 1 + \frac{1}{6} = 4\frac{1}{6}$

Your Turn!	1) $2\frac{1}{15} + 1\frac{2}{5} = 3\frac{7}{15}$	2) $1\frac{3}{10} + 3\frac{1}{5} = 4\frac{1}{2}$
	3) $1\frac{1}{10} + 2\frac{2}{5} = 3\frac{1}{2}$	4) $2\frac{5}{6} + 2\frac{2}{9} = 5\frac{1}{18}$
Find more at bit.ly/2M4oABB	5) $2\frac{2}{7} + 1\frac{2}{21} = 3\frac{8}{21}$	6) $1\frac{3}{8} + 3\frac{2}{3} = 5\frac{1}{24}$
	7) $1\frac{1}{6} + 4\frac{2}{7} = 5\frac{19}{42}$	8) $2\frac{1}{6} + 1\frac{2}{5} = 3\frac{17}{30}$

Topic	**Subtracting Mixed Numbers**
Notes	Use the following steps for subtracting mixed numbers. ✓ Convert mixed numbers into improper fractions. $a\frac{c}{b} = \frac{ab+c}{b}$ ✓ Find equivalent fractions with the same denominator for unlike fractions (fractions with different denominators) ✓ Subtract the second fraction from the first one. ✓ Write your answer in lowest terms and convert it into a mixed number if the answer is an improper fraction.
Example	**Subtract.** $5\frac{1}{2} - 2\frac{2}{3} =$ Convert mixed numbers into fractions: $5\frac{1}{2} = \frac{5\times2+1}{2} = \frac{11}{2}$ and $2\frac{2}{3} = \frac{2\times3+2}{3} = \frac{8}{3}$, these two fractions are "unlike" fractions. (they have different denominators). Find equivalent fractions with the same denominator. Use this formula: $\frac{a}{b} - \frac{c}{d} = \frac{ad-bc}{bd}$ $\frac{11}{2} - \frac{8}{3} = \frac{(11)(3)-(2)(8)}{2\times3} = \frac{33-16}{6} = \frac{17}{6}$, the answer is an improper fraction, convert it into a mixed number. $\frac{17}{6} = 2\frac{5}{6}$
Your Turn!	1) $3\frac{1}{4} - 1\frac{2}{3} =$ \qquad 2) $4\frac{4}{9} - 1\frac{1}{3} =$
	3) $6\frac{1}{4} - 1\frac{2}{7} =$ \qquad 4) $8\frac{2}{3} - 1\frac{1}{4} =$
Find more at bit.ly/3aD3KDG	5) $8\frac{3}{4} - 1\frac{3}{8} =$ \qquad 6) $2\frac{3}{8} - 1\frac{2}{3} =$
	7) $8\frac{3}{5} - 1\frac{2}{25} =$ \qquad 8) $5\frac{2}{3} - 2\frac{4}{7} =$

Topic	**Subtracting Mixed Numbers - Answers**
Notes	Use the following steps for subtracting mixed numbers. ✓ Convert mixed numbers into improper fractions. $a\frac{c}{b} = \frac{ab+c}{b}$ ✓ Find equivalent fractions with the same denominator for unlike fractions (fractions with different denominators) ✓ Subtract the second fraction from the first one. ✓ Write your answer in lowest terms and convert it into a mixed number if the answer is an improper fraction.
Example	***Subtract.*** $5\frac{1}{2} - 2\frac{2}{3} =$ Convert mixed numbers into fractions: $5\frac{1}{2} = \frac{5 \times 2 + 1}{2} = \frac{11}{2}$ and $2\frac{2}{3} = \frac{2 \times 3 + 2}{3} = \frac{8}{3}$, these two fractions are "unlike" fractions. (they have different denominators). Find equivalent fractions with the same denominator. Use this formula: $\frac{a}{b} - \frac{c}{d} = \frac{ad - bc}{bd}$ $\frac{11}{2} - \frac{8}{3} = \frac{(11)(3) - (2)(8)}{2 \times 3} = \frac{33 - 16}{6} = \frac{17}{6}$, the answer is an improper fraction, convert it into a mixed number. $\frac{17}{6} = 2\frac{5}{6}$

Your Turn!	1) $3\frac{1}{4} - 1\frac{2}{3} = 1\frac{7}{12}$	2) $4\frac{4}{9} - 1\frac{1}{3} = 3\frac{1}{9}$
	3) $6\frac{1}{4} - 1\frac{2}{7} = 4\frac{27}{28}$	4) $8\frac{2}{3} - 1\frac{1}{4} = 7\frac{5}{12}$
Find more at bit.ly/3aD3KDG	5) $8\frac{3}{4} - 1\frac{3}{8} = 7\frac{3}{8}$	6) $2\frac{3}{8} - 1\frac{2}{3} = \frac{17}{24}$
	7) $8\frac{3}{5} - 1\frac{2}{25} = 7\frac{13}{25}$	8) $5\frac{2}{3} - 2\frac{4}{7} = 3\frac{2}{21}$

Topic	**Multiplying Mixed Numbers**
Notes	✓ Convert the mixed numbers into fractions. $a\dfrac{c}{b} = a + \dfrac{c}{b} = \dfrac{ab+c}{b}$ ✓ Multiply fractions and simplify if necessary. $\dfrac{a}{b} \times \dfrac{c}{d} = \dfrac{a \times c}{b \times d}$ ✓ If the answer is an improper fraction (numerator is bigger than denominator), convert it into a mixed number.
Example	***Multiply*** $2\dfrac{1}{4} \times 3\dfrac{1}{2}$ Convert mixed numbers into fractions: $2\dfrac{1}{4} = \dfrac{2 \times 4 + 1}{4} = \dfrac{9}{4}$ and $3\dfrac{1}{2} = \dfrac{3 \times 2 + 1}{2} = \dfrac{7}{2}$ Multiply two fractions: $\dfrac{9}{4} \times \dfrac{7}{2} = \dfrac{9 \times 7}{4 \times 2} = \dfrac{63}{8}$ The answer is an improper fraction. Convert it into a mixed number: $$\dfrac{63}{8} = 7\dfrac{7}{8}$$
Your Turn! **Find more at** bit.ly/3aPy7XJ	1) $3\dfrac{1}{3} \times 4\dfrac{1}{8} =$ 2) $5\dfrac{1}{2} \times 2\dfrac{6}{7} =$ 3) $3\dfrac{1}{3} \times 3\dfrac{3}{4} =$ 4) $2\dfrac{2}{9} \times 6\dfrac{1}{3} =$ 5) $2\dfrac{2}{7} \times 4\dfrac{3}{5} =$ 6) $1\dfrac{4}{7} \times 9\dfrac{1}{2} =$ 7) $3\dfrac{3}{5} \times 4\dfrac{1}{3} =$ 8) $5\dfrac{1}{4} \times 1\dfrac{1}{7} =$

Topic	Multiplying Mixed Numbers - Answers
Notes	✓ Convert the mixed numbers into fractions. $a\frac{c}{b} = a + \frac{c}{b} = \frac{ab+c}{b}$ ✓ Multiply fractions and simplify if necessary. $\frac{a}{b} \times \frac{c}{d} = \frac{a \times c}{b \times d}$ ✓ If the answer is an improper fraction (numerator is bigger than denominator), convert it into a mixed number.
Example	***Multiply*** $2\frac{1}{4} \times 3\frac{1}{2}$ Convert mixed numbers into fractions: $2\frac{1}{4} = \frac{2 \times 4 + 1}{4} = \frac{9}{4}$ and $3\frac{1}{2} = \frac{3 \times 2 + 1}{2} = \frac{7}{2}$ Multiply two fractions: $\frac{9}{4} \times \frac{7}{2} = \frac{9 \times 7}{4 \times 2} = \frac{63}{8}$ The answer is an improper fraction. Convert it into a mixed number: $$\frac{63}{8} = 7\frac{7}{8}$$

Your Turn!		
	1) $3\frac{1}{3} \times 4\frac{1}{8} = 13\frac{3}{4}$	2) $5\frac{1}{2} \times 2\frac{6}{7} = 15\frac{5}{7}$
	3) $3\frac{1}{3} \times 3\frac{3}{4} = 12\frac{1}{2}$	4) $2\frac{2}{9} \times 6\frac{1}{3} = 14\frac{2}{27}$
Find more at bit.ly/3aPy7XJ	5) $2\frac{2}{7} \times 4\frac{3}{5} = 10\frac{18}{35}$	6) $1\frac{4}{7} \times 9\frac{1}{2} = 14\frac{13}{14}$
	7) $3\frac{3}{5} \times 4\frac{1}{3} = 15\frac{3}{5}$	8) $5\frac{1}{4} \times 1\frac{1}{7} = 6$

Topic	**Dividing Mixed Numbers**
Notes	✓ Convert the mixed numbers into improper fractions. $$a\frac{c}{b} = a + \frac{c}{b} = \frac{ab+c}{b}$$ ✓ Divide fractions and simplify if necessary.
Example	*Solve.* $2\frac{1}{3} \div 1\frac{1}{4} =$ Converting mixed numbers to fractions: $2\frac{1}{3} \div 1\frac{1}{4} = \frac{7}{3} \div \frac{5}{4}$ Keep, Change, Flip: $\frac{7}{3} \div \frac{5}{4} = \frac{7}{3} \times \frac{4}{5} = \frac{7 \times 4}{3 \times 5} = \frac{28}{15} = 1\frac{13}{15}$

Your Turn!		
	1) $2\frac{4}{7} \div 1\frac{1}{5} =$	2) $3\frac{3}{10} \div 2\frac{5}{8} =$
	3) $4\frac{2}{3} \div 3\frac{2}{5} =$	4) $5\frac{4}{5} \div 4\frac{3}{4} =$
	5) $1\frac{8}{9} \div 2\frac{3}{7} =$	6) $3\frac{3}{8} \div 2\frac{2}{5} =$
	7) $4\frac{1}{5} \div 3\frac{1}{9} =$	8) $4\frac{2}{3} \div 1\frac{8}{9} =$
	9) $4\frac{1}{6} \div 3\frac{2}{3} =$	10) $6\frac{1}{3} \div 4\frac{1}{6} =$

Find more at

bit.ly/2KLPk9k

Topic	Dividing Mixed Numbers- Answers
Notes	✓ Convert the mixed numbers into improper fractions. $$a\frac{c}{b} = a + \frac{c}{b} = \frac{ab + c}{b}$$ ✓ Divide fractions and simplify if necessary.
Example	***Solve.*** $2\frac{1}{3} \div 1\frac{1}{4} =$ Converting mixed numbers to fractions: $2\frac{1}{3} \div 1\frac{1}{4} = \frac{7}{3} \div \frac{5}{4}$ Keep, Change, Flip: $\frac{7}{3} \div \frac{5}{4} = \frac{7}{3} \times \frac{4}{5} = \frac{7 \times 4}{3 \times 5} = \frac{28}{15} = 1\frac{13}{15}$

Your Turn!		
	1) $2\frac{4}{7} \div 1\frac{1}{5} = 2\frac{1}{7}$	2) $3\frac{3}{10} \div 2\frac{5}{8} = 1\frac{9}{35}$
	3) $4\frac{2}{3} \div 3\frac{2}{5} = 1\frac{19}{51}$	4) $5\frac{4}{5} \div 4\frac{3}{4} = 1\frac{21}{95}$
	5) $1\frac{8}{9} \div 2\frac{3}{7} = \frac{7}{9}$	6) $3\frac{3}{8} \div 2\frac{2}{5} = 1\frac{13}{32}$
Find more at bit.ly/2KLPk9k	7) $4\frac{1}{5} \div 3\frac{1}{9} = 1\frac{7}{20}$	8) $4\frac{2}{3} \div 1\frac{8}{9} = 2\frac{8}{17}$
	9) $4\frac{1}{6} \div 3\frac{2}{3} = 1\frac{3}{22}$	10) $6\frac{1}{3} \div 4\frac{1}{6} = 1\frac{13}{25}$

Topic	**Comparing Decimals**
Notes	Decimals: is a fraction written in a special form. For example, instead of writing $\frac{1}{2}$ you can write 0.5. For comparing decimals: ✓ Compare each digit of two decimals in the same place value. ✓ Start from left. Compare hundreds, tens, ones, tenth, hundredth, etc. ✓ To compare numbers, use these symbols: - Equal to =, Less than <, Greater than > Greater than or equal ≥, Less than or equal ≤
Examples	***Compare*** $\mathbf{0.40}$ ***and*** $\mathbf{0.04}$. 0.40 *is greater than* 0.04, because the tenth place of 0.40 is 4, but the tenth place of 0.04 is zero. Then: $0.40 > 0.04$ ***Compare*** $\mathbf{0.0912}$ ***and*** $\mathbf{0.912}$. 0.912 *is greater than* 0.0912, because the tenth place of 0.912 is 9, but the tenth place of 0.0912 is zero. Then: $0.0912 < 0.912$

Your Turn!	1) 0.32 ☐ 0.36	2) 1.68 ☐ 1.70
	3) 19.1 ☐ 19.09	4) 2.45 ☐ 2.089
	5) 1.258 ☐ 12.58	6) 0.89 ☐ 0.890
Find more at bit.ly/2WHt2Za	7) 2.657 ☐ 3.568	8) 0.368 ☐ 0.683

Topic	Comparing Decimals – Answers
Notes	Decimals: is a fraction written in a special form. For example, instead of writing $\frac{1}{2}$ you can write 0.5. For comparing decimals: ✓ Compare each digit of two decimals in the same place value. ✓ Start from left. Compare hundreds, tens, ones, tenth, hundredth, etc. ✓ To compare numbers, use these symbols: - Equal to =, Less than <, Greater than > Greater than or equal ≥, Less than or equal ≤
Examples	***Compare 0.40 and 0.04.*** 0.40 *is greater than* 0.04, because the tenth place of 0.40 is 4, but the tenth place of 0.04 is zero. Then: $0.40 > 0.04$ ***Compare 0.0912 and 0.912.*** 0.912 *is greater than* 0.0912, because the tenth place of 0.912 is 9, but the tenth place of 0.0912 is zero. Then: $0.0912 < 0.912$

Your Turn!		
	1) $0.32 < 0.36$	2) $1.68 < 1.70$
	3) $19.1 > 19.09$	4) $2.45 > 2.089$
	5) $1.258 < 12.58$	6) $0.89 = 0.890$
Find more at bit.ly/2WHt2Za	7) $2.657 < 3.568$	8) $0.368 < 0.683$

Topic	**Rounding Decimals**
Notes	✓ We can round decimals to a certain accuracy or number of decimal places. ✓ Let's review place values: For example: 35.4817 3: tens 5: ones 4: tenths 8: hundredths 1: thousandths 7:tens thousandths ✓ To round a decimal, find the place value you'll round to. ✓ Find the digit to the right of the place value you're rounding to. If it is 5 or bigger, add 1 to the place value you're rounding to and remove all digits on its right side. If the digit to the right of the place value is less than 5, keep the place value and remove all digits on the right.
Example	***Round 12.8365 to the hundredth place value.*** First look at the next place value to the right, (thousandths). It's 6 and it is greater than 5. Thus add 1 to the digit in the hundredth place. It is 3. → 3 + 1 = 4, then, the answer is 12.84

Your Turn!	*Round each number to the underlined place value.*	
	1) 23.5<u>6</u>3=	2) 1.2<u>2</u>3=
	3) 55.<u>4</u>23 =	4) 2<u>5</u>.62 =
	5) 11.<u>2</u>65 =	6) 33.5<u>0</u>5 =
Find more at bit.ly/3mKEluf	7) 4.4<u>8</u>3=	8) 9.0<u>1</u>8=

Topic	**Rounding Decimals – Answers**
Notes	✓ We can round decimals to a certain accuracy or number of decimal places. ✓ Let's review place values: For example: 35.4817 3: tens 5: ones 4: tenths 8: hundredths 1: thousandths 7:tens thousandths ✓ To round a decimal, find the place value you'll round to. ✓ Find the digit to the right of the place value you're rounding to. If it is 5 or bigger, add 1 to the place value you're rounding to and remove all digits on its right side. If the digit to the right of the place value is less than 5, keep the place value and remove all digits on the right.
Example	**Round 12.8365 *to the hundredth place value.*** First look at the next place value to the right, (thousandths). It's 6 and it is greater than 5. Thus add 1 to the digit in the hundredth place. It is 3. $\rightarrow 3 + 1 = 4$, then, the answer is 12.84

Your Turn!	*Round each number to the underlined place value.*	
Find more at bit.ly/3mKEluf	1) 23.5$\underline{6}$3 = 23.56	2) 1.2$\underline{2}$3 = 1.22
	3) 55.$\underline{4}$23 = 55.4	4) 2$\underline{5}$.62 = 26
	5) 11.$\underline{2}$65 = 11.3	6) 33.5$\underline{0}$5 = 33.51
	7) 4.4$\underline{8}$3 = 4.48	8) 9.0$\underline{1}$8 = 9.02

Topic	**Adding and Subtracting Decimals**
Notes	✓ Line up the numbers. ✓ Add zeros to have same number of digits for both numbers if necessary. ✓ Add or subtract using column addition or subtraction.
Examples	**Add**. $2.6 + 5.33 =$ First line up the numbers: $\begin{array}{r} 2.6 \\ +\,5.33 \\ \hline \end{array}$ →Add zeros to have same number of digits for both numbers. $\begin{array}{r} 2.60 \\ +\,5.33 \\ \hline \end{array}$ → Start with the hundredths place. $0 + 3 = 3$, $\begin{array}{r} 2.60 \\ +\,5.33 \\ \hline 3 \end{array}$ → Continue with tenths place. $6 + 3 = 9$, $\begin{array}{r} 2.60 \\ +\,5.33 \\ \hline .93 \end{array}$ → Add the ones place. $2 + 5 = 7$, $\begin{array}{r} 2.60 \\ +\,5.33 \\ \hline 7.93 \end{array}$ **Subtract**. $4.79 - 3.13 =$ $\begin{array}{r} 4.79 \\ -\,3.13 \\ \hline \end{array}$ Start with the hundredths place. $9 - 3 = 6$, $\begin{array}{r} 4.79 \\ -\,3.13 \\ \hline 6 \end{array}$, continue with tenths place. $7 - 1 = 6$, $\begin{array}{r} 4.79 \\ -\,3.13 \\ \hline .66 \end{array}$, subtract the ones place. $4 - 3 = 1$, $\begin{array}{r} 4.79 \\ -\,3.13 \\ \hline 1.66 \end{array}$
Your Turn!	1) $28.15 + 16.58 =$ 2) $65.36 - 56.16 =$
	3) $38.19 + 24.18 =$ 4) $57.26 - 43.54 =$
Find more at bit.ly/38uyUdx	5) $21.67 + 37.91 =$ 6) $39.58 - 26.44 =$

Topic	Adding and Subtracting Decimals - Answers
Notes	✓ Line up the numbers. ✓ Add zeros to have same number of digits for both numbers if necessary. ✓ Add or subtract using column addition or subtraction.
Examples	**Add**. $2.6 + 5.33 =$ First line up the numbers: $\begin{array}{r} 2.6 \\ + 5.33 \\ \hline \end{array}$ →Add zeros to have same number of digits for both numbers. $\begin{array}{r} 2.60 \\ + 5.33 \\ \hline \end{array}$ → Start with the hundredths place. $0 + 3 = 3$, $\begin{array}{r} 2.60 \\ + 5.33 \\ \hline 3 \end{array}$ → Continue with tenths place. $6 + 3 = 9$, $\begin{array}{r} 2.60 \\ + 5.33 \\ \hline .93 \end{array}$ → Add the ones place. $2 + 5 = 7$, $\begin{array}{r} 2.60 \\ + 5.33 \\ \hline 7.93 \end{array}$ **Subtract**. $4.79 - 3.13 =$ $\begin{array}{r} 4.79 \\ - 3.13 \\ \hline \end{array}$ Start with the hundredths place. $9 - 3 = 6$, $\begin{array}{r} 4.79 \\ - 3.13 \\ \hline 6 \end{array}$, continue with tenths place. $7 - 1 = 6$, $\begin{array}{r} 4.79 \\ - 3.13 \\ \hline .66 \end{array}$, subtract the ones place. $4 - 3 = 1$, $\begin{array}{r} 4.79 \\ - 3.13 \\ \hline 1.66 \end{array}$

Your Turn!	1) $28.15 + 16.58 = 44.73$	2) $65.36 - 56.16 = 9.20$
	3) $38.19 + 24.18 = 62.37$	4) $57.26 - 43.54 = 13.72$
Find more at bit.ly/38uyUdx	5) $21.67 + 37.91 = 59.58$	6) $39.58 - 26.44 = 13.14$

Topic	Multiplying and Dividing Decimals
Notes	For Multiplication: ✓ Ignore the decimal point and set up and multiply the numbers as you do with whole numbers. ✓ Count the total number of decimal places in both factors. ✓ Place the decimal point in the product. For Division: ✓ If the divisor is not a whole number, move decimal point to right to make it a whole number. Do the same for dividend. ✓ Divide similar to whole numbers.
Examples	***Find the product.*** $1.2 \times 2.3 =$ Set up and multiply the numbers as you do with whole numbers. Line up the numbers: $\begin{smallmatrix}12\\ \times 23\end{smallmatrix}$ → Multiply: $\frac{\begin{smallmatrix}12\\ \times 23\end{smallmatrix}}{276}$ → Count the total number of decimal places in both of the factors. There are two decimal digits. Then: $1.2 \times 2.3 = 2.76$ ***Find the quotient.*** $5.6 \div 0.8 =$ The divisor is not a whole number. Multiply it by 10 to get 8. → $0.8 \times 10 = 8$ Do the same for the dividend to get 56 → $5.6 \times 10 = 56$ Now, divide: $56 \div 8 = 7$. The answer is 7.
Your Turn! **Find more at** bit.ly/34DZ0cS	1) $1.16 \times 0.5 =$ ⫿ 2) $45.5 \div 5 =$
	3) $0.9 \times 0.68 =$ ⫿ 4) $66.8 \div 0.2 =$
	5) $0.16 \times 0.4 =$ ⫿ 6) $58.9 \div 100 =$

Topic	**Multiplying and Dividing Decimals – Answers**
Notes	For Multiplication: ✓ Ignore the decimal point and set up and multiply the numbers as you do with whole numbers. ✓ Count the total number of decimal places in both factors. ✓ Place the decimal point in the product. For Division: ✓ If the divisor is not a whole number, move decimal point to right to make it a whole number. Do the same for dividend. ✓ Divide similar to whole numbers.
Examples	***Find the product.*** $1.2 \times 2.3 =$ Set up and multiply the numbers as you do with whole numbers. Line up the numbers: $\overset{12}{\underset{}{\times 23}}$ → Multiply: $\overset{12}{\underset{276}{\times 23}}$ → Count the total number of decimal places in both of the factors. There are two decimal digits. Then: $1.2 \times 2.3 = 2.76$ ***Find the quotient.*** $5.6 \div 0.8 =$ The divisor is not a whole number. Multiply it by 10 to get 8. → $0.8 \times 10 = 8$ Do the same for the dividend to get 56 → $5.6 \times 10 = 56$ Now, divide: $56 \div 8 = 7$. The answer is 7.

Your Turn!	1) $1.16 \times 0.5 = 0.58$	2) $45.5 \div 5 = 9.1$
	3) $0.9 \times 0.68 = 0.612$	4) $66.8 \div 0.2 = 334$
Find more at bit.ly/34DZ0cS	5) $0.16 \times 0.4 = 0.064$	6) $58.9 \div 100 = 0.589$

Topic	Adding and Subtracting Integers
Notes	✓ Integers include: zero, counting numbers, and the negative of the counting numbers. $\{\ldots, -3, -2, -1, 0, 1, 2, 3, \ldots\}$ ✓ Add a positive integer by moving to the right on the number line. ✓ Add a negative integer by moving to the left on the number line. Subtract an integer by adding its opposite.
Examples	*Solve.* $(4) - (-8) =$ Keep the first number and convert the sign of the second number to its opposite. (change subtraction into addition. Then: $(4) + 8 = 12$ *Solve.* $42 + (12 - 26) =$ First subtract the numbers in brackets, $12 - 26 = -14$ Then: $42 + (-14) = \rightarrow$ change addition into subtraction: $42 - 14 = 28$

Your Turn!	1) $-(13) + 10 =$	2) $(-6) + (-11) + 15 =$
	3) $(-13) + 7 =$	4) $3 - (-7) + 14 =$
	5) $(-7) + (-8) =$	6) $16 - (-4 + 8) =$
Find more at bit.ly/3aKx5vl	7) $2 + (-6) + 8 =$	8) $-(19) - (-6) + 3 =$

Topic	Adding and Subtracting Integers – Answers
Notes	✓ Integers include: zero, counting numbers, and the negative of the counting numbers. $\{... , -3, -2, -1, 0, 1, 2, 3, ...\}$ ✓ Add a positive integer by moving to the right on the number line. ✓ Add a negative integer by moving to the left on the number line. Subtract an integer by adding its opposite.
Examples	**Solve.** $(4) - (-8) =$ Keep the first number and convert the sign of the second number to its opposite. (change subtraction into addition. Then: $(4) + 8 = 12$ **Solve.** $42 + (12 - 26) =$ First subtract the numbers in brackets, $12 - 26 = -14$ Then: $42 + (-14) = \rightarrow$ change addition into subtraction: $42 - 14 = 28$

Your Turn!	1) $-(13) + 10 = -3$	2) $(-6) + (-11) + 15 = -2$
	3) $(-13) + 7 = -6$	4) $3 - (-7) + 14 = 24$
	5) $(-7) + (-8) = -15$	6) $16 - (-4 + 8) = 12$
Find more at bit.ly/3aKx5vl	7) $2 + (-6) + 8 = 4$	8) $-(19) - (-6) + 3 = -10$

Topic	**Multiplying and Dividing Integers**
Notes	Use following rules for multiplying and dividing integers: ✓ (negative) × (negative) = positive ✓ (negative) ÷ (negative) = positive ✓ (negative) × (positive) = negative ✓ (negative) ÷ (positive) = negative ✓ (positive) × (positive) = positive ✓ (positive) ÷ (negative) = negative

Examples	***Solve.*** $2 \times (14 - 17) =$
	    First subtract the numbers in brackets, $14 - 17 = -3 \rightarrow (2) \times (-3) =$
	    Now use this rule: (positive) × (negative) = negative
	    $(2) \times (-3) = -6$
	
	Solve. $(-7) + (-36 \div 4) =$
	    First divide -36 by 4, the numbers in brackets, using this rule:
	    (negative) ÷ (positive) = negative
	    Then: $-36 \div 4 = -9$. Now, add -7 and -9:
	            $(-7) + (-9) = -7 - 9 = -16$

Your Turn!	1) $(-4) \times 3 =$ 2) $(-48) \div (-8) =$
	3) $(-11) \times (-3) =$ 4) $81 \div (-9) =$
	5) $(15 - 12) \times (-7) =$ 6) $(-12) \div (3) =$
	7) $3 \times (-7) =$ 8) $(9) \div (-3) =$

Find more at

bit.ly/3pjQW98

Topic	Multiplying and Dividing Integers - Answers
Notes	Use following rules for multiplying and dividing integers: ✓ (negative) × (negative) = positive ✓ (negative) ÷ (negative) = positive ✓ (negative) × (positive) = negative ✓ (negative) ÷ (positive) = negative ✓ (positive) × (positive) = positive ✓ (positive) ÷ (negative) = negative
Examples	***Solve.*** $2 \times (14 - 17) =$ First subtract the numbers in brackets, $14 - 17 = -3 \rightarrow (2) \times (-3) =$ Now use this rule: (positive) × (negative) = negative $(2) \times (-3) = -6$ ***Solve.*** $(-7) + (-36 \div 4) =$ First divide -36 by 4, the numbers in brackets, using this rule: (negative) ÷ (positive) = negative Then: $-36 \div 4 = -9$. Now, add -7 and -9: $(-7) + (-9) = -7 - 9 = -16$

Your Turn!		
	1) $(-4) \times 3 = -12$	2) $(-48) \div (-8) = 6$
	3) $(-11) \times (-3) = 33$	4) $81 \div (-9) = -9$
Find more at bit.ly/3pjQW98	5) $(15 - 12) \times (-7) =$ -21	6) $(-12) \div (3) = -4$
	7) $3 \times (-7) = -21$	8) $(9) \div (-3) = -3$

Topic	Order of Operation
Notes	When there is more than one math operation, use PEMDAS: (to memorize this rule, remember the phrase "Please Excuse My Dear Aunt Sally") ✓ Parentheses ✓ Exponents ✓ Multiplication and Division (from left to right) ✓ Addition and Subtraction (from left to right)
Examples	***Calculate***. $(18 - 26) \div (2^4 \div 4) =$ First simplify inside parentheses: $(-8) \div (16 \div 4) = (-8) \div (4)$ Then: $(-8) \div (4) = -2$ ***Solve***. $(-5 \times 7) - (18 - 3^2) =$ First calculate within parentheses: $(-5 \times 7) - (18 - 3^2) = (-35) - (18 - 9)$ Then: $(-35) - (18 - 9) = -35 - 9 = -44$

Your Turn!		
	1) $(12 \times 3) \div (6 + 6) =$	2) $(36 \div 4) + (11 - 4) =$
	3) $(-9) + (5 \times 6) + 14 =$	4) $(-10 \times 5) \div (2^2 + 1) =$
	5) $[-16(32 \div 2^3)] \div 8 =$	6) $(-7) + (72 \div 3^2) + 12 =$
	7) $[10(64 \div 2^4)] - 3^2 =$	8) $3^3 + (-6 \times 2^3) + 4 =$

Find more at

bit.ly/37LBw7X

Topic	Order of Operation – Answers
Notes	When there is more than one math operation, use PEMDAS: (to memorize this rule, remember the phrase "Please Excuse My Dear Aunt Sally") ✓ Parentheses ✓ Exponents ✓ Multiplication and Division (from left to right) ✓ Addition and Subtraction (from left to right)
Examples	***Calculate.*** $(18 - 26) \div (2^4 \div 4) =$ First simplify inside parentheses: $(-8) \div (16 \div 4) = (-8) \div (4)$ Then: $(-8) \div (4) = -2$ ***Solve.*** $(-5 \times 7) - (18 - 3^2) =$ First calculate within parentheses: $(-5 \times 7) - (18 - 3^2) = (-35) - (18 - 9)$ Then: $(-35) - (18 - 9) = -35 - 9 = -44$

Your Turn!	1) $(12 \times 3) \div (6 + 6) = 3$	2) $(36 \div 4) + (11 - 4) = 16$
	3) $(-9) + (5 \times 6) + 14 = 35$	4) $(-10 \times 5) \div (2^2 + 1) = -10$
	5) $[-16(32 \div 2^3)] \div 8 = -8$	6) $(-7) + (72 \div 3^2) + 12 = 13$
Find more at bit.ly/37LBw7X	7) $[10(64 \div 2^4)] - 3^2 =$ 31	8) $3^3 + (-6 \times 2^3) + 4 = -17$

Topic	Integers and Absolute Value
Notes	✓ The absolute value of a number is its distance from zero, in either direction, on the number line. For example, the distance of 9 and -9 from zero on number line is 9. ✓ Absolute value is symbolized by vertical bars, as in $\lvert x \rvert$.
Example	***Calculate.*** $\lvert 8-5 \rvert \times \lvert 12-16 \rvert =$ First calculate $\lvert 8-5 \rvert$, $\rightarrow \lvert 8-5 \rvert = \lvert 3 \rvert$, the absolute value of 3 is 3, $\lvert 3 \rvert = 3$ $8 \times \lvert 12-16 \rvert =$ Now calculate $\lvert 12-16 \rvert$, $\rightarrow \lvert 12-16 \rvert = \lvert -4 \rvert$, the absolute value of -4 is 4, $\lvert -4 \rvert = 4$. Then: $3 \times 4 = 12$

Your Turn!

1) $12 - \lvert 6-15 \rvert =$

2) $12 - \lvert 14-18 \rvert - \lvert 6 \rvert =$

3) $\lvert 21 \rvert - \frac{\lvert -25 \rvert}{5} =$

4) $\lvert 30 \rvert + \frac{\lvert -49 \rvert}{7} =$

5) $\frac{\lvert 7 \times -8 \rvert}{4} \times \frac{\lvert -12 \rvert}{2} =$

6) $\frac{\lvert 10 \times -6 \rvert}{5} \times \lvert -9 \rvert =$

7) $\frac{\lvert -45 \rvert}{9} \times \frac{\lvert -42 \rvert}{7} =$

8) $\lvert -25+4 \rvert \times \frac{\lvert -8 \times 3 \rvert}{6} =$

Find more at
bit.ly/3aD521u

Topic	Integers and Absolute Value – Answers
Notes	✓ The absolute value of a number is its distance from zero, in either direction, on the number line. For example, the distance of 9 and -9 from zero on number line is 9. ✓ Absolute value is symbolized by vertical bars, as in $\lvert x \rvert$.
Example	***Calculate.*** $\lvert 8 - 5 \rvert \times \lvert 12 - 16 \rvert =$ First calculate $\lvert 8 - 5 \rvert$, $\rightarrow \lvert 8 - 5 \rvert = \lvert 3 \rvert$, the absolute value of 3 is 3, $\lvert 3 \rvert = 3$ $8 \times \lvert 12 - 16 \rvert =$ Now calculate $\lvert 12 - 16 \rvert$, $\rightarrow \lvert 12 - 16 \rvert = \lvert -4 \rvert$, the absolute value of -4 is 4, $\lvert -4 \rvert = 4$. Then: $3 \times 4 = 12$

Your Turn!	1) $12 - \lvert 6 - 15 \rvert = 3$	2) $12 - \lvert 14 - 18 \rvert - \lvert 6 \rvert = 2$
	3) $\lvert 21 \rvert - \dfrac{\lvert -25 \rvert}{5} = 16$	4) $\lvert 30 \rvert + \dfrac{\lvert -49 \rvert}{7} = 37$
	5) $\dfrac{\lvert 7 \times -8 \rvert}{4} \times \dfrac{\lvert -12 \rvert}{2} = 84$	6) $\dfrac{\lvert 10 \times -6 \rvert}{5} \times \lvert -9 \rvert = 108$
Find more at bit.ly/3aD521u	7) $\dfrac{\lvert -45 \rvert}{9} \times \dfrac{\lvert -42 \rvert}{7} = 30$	8) $\lvert -25 + 4 \rvert \times \dfrac{\lvert -8 \times 3 \rvert}{6} = 84$

Topic	Simplifying Ratios
Notes	✓ Ratios are used to make comparisons between two numbers. ✓ Ratios can be written as a fraction, using the word "to", or with a colon. ✓ You can calculate equivalent ratios by multiplying or dividing both sides of the ratio by the same number.
Examples	***Simplify.*** $18:63 =$ Both numbers 18 and 63 are divisible by $9 \Rightarrow 18 \div 9 = 2$, $63 \div 9 = 7$, Then: $18:63 = 2:7$ ***Simplify.*** $\frac{25}{45} =$ Both numbers 25 and 45 are divisible by 5, $\Rightarrow 25 \div 5 = 5$, $45 \div 5 = 9$, Then: $\frac{25}{45} = \frac{5}{9}$

Your Turn!	1) $\frac{6}{48} = -$	2) $\frac{35}{60} = -$
	3) $\frac{15}{35} = -$	4) $\frac{42}{54} = -$
	5) $\frac{12}{36} = -$	6) $\frac{30}{80} = -$
Find more at bit.ly/3nKwq0Z	7) $\frac{16}{36} = -$	8) $\frac{30}{108} = -$

Topic	Simplifying Ratios – Answers
Notes	✓ Ratios are used to make comparisons between two numbers. ✓ Ratios can be written as a fraction, using the word "to", or with a colon. ✓ You can calculate equivalent ratios by multiplying or dividing both sides of the ratio by the same number.
Examples	***Simplify.*** $18:63 =$ Both numbers 18 and 63 are divisible by $9 \Rightarrow 18 \div 9 = 2, 63 \div 9 = 7$, Then: $18:63 = 2:7$ ***Simplify.*** $\frac{25}{45} =$ Both numbers 25 and 45 are divisible by $5, \Rightarrow 25 \div 5 = 5, 45 \div 5 = 9$, Then: $\frac{25}{45} = \frac{5}{9}$

Your Turn!	1) $\frac{6}{48} = \frac{1}{8}$	2) $\frac{35}{60} = \frac{7}{12}$
	3) $\frac{15}{35} = \frac{3}{7}$	4) $\frac{42}{54} = \frac{7}{9}$
	5) $\frac{12}{36} = \frac{1}{3}$	6) $\frac{30}{80} = \frac{3}{8}$
Find more at bit.ly/3nKwq0Z	7) $\frac{16}{36} = \frac{4}{9}$	8) $\frac{30}{108} = \frac{5}{18}$

Topic	Proportional Ratios
Notes	✓ Two ratios are proportional if they represent the same relationship. ✓ A proportion means that two ratios are equal. It can be written in two ways: $\dfrac{a}{b} = \dfrac{c}{d}$ $a : b = c : d$
Example	**Solve this proportion for** x. $\dfrac{5}{8} = \dfrac{35}{x}$ Use cross multiplication: $\dfrac{5}{8} = \dfrac{35}{x} \Rightarrow 5 \times x = 8 \times 35 \Rightarrow 5x = 280$ Divide to find x: $x = \dfrac{280}{5} \Rightarrow x = 56$

Your Turn!		
	1) $\dfrac{1}{3} = \dfrac{7}{x} \Rightarrow x = $ _____	2) $\dfrac{4}{3} = \dfrac{20}{x} \Rightarrow x = $ _____
	3) $\dfrac{3}{11} = \dfrac{6}{x} \Rightarrow x = $ _____	4) $\dfrac{12}{20} = \dfrac{x}{200} \Rightarrow x = $ _____
	5) $\dfrac{9}{12} = \dfrac{27}{x} \Rightarrow x = $ _____	6) $\dfrac{14}{16} = \dfrac{x}{80} \Rightarrow x = $ _____
Find more at bit.ly/37GHQxp	7) $\dfrac{5}{14} = \dfrac{40}{x} \Rightarrow x = $ _____	8) $\dfrac{8}{12} = \dfrac{36}{x} \Rightarrow x = $ _____

Topic	**Proportional Ratios - Answers**
Notes	✓ Two ratios are proportional if they represent the same relationship. ✓ A proportion means that two ratios are equal. It can be written in two ways: $\frac{a}{b} = \frac{c}{d}$ $\qquad$ $a : b = c : d$
Example	*Solve this proportion for* x. $\frac{5}{8} = \frac{35}{x}$ Use cross multiplication: $\frac{5}{8} = \frac{35}{x} \Rightarrow 5 \times x = 8 \times 35 \Rightarrow 5x = 280$ Divide to find x: $\quad x = \frac{280}{5} \Rightarrow x = 56$

Your Turn!		
	1) $\frac{1}{3} = \frac{7}{x} \Rightarrow x = 21$	2) $\frac{4}{3} = \frac{20}{x} \Rightarrow x = 15$
	3) $\frac{3}{11} = \frac{6}{x} \Rightarrow x = 22$	4) $\frac{12}{20} = \frac{x}{200} \Rightarrow x = 120$
	5) $\frac{9}{12} = \frac{27}{x} \Rightarrow x = 36$	6) $\frac{14}{16} = \frac{x}{80} \Rightarrow x = 70$
Find more at bit.ly/37GHQxp	7) $\frac{5}{14} = \frac{40}{x} \Rightarrow x = 112$	8) $\frac{8}{12} = \frac{36}{x} \Rightarrow x = 54$

Topic	Create Proportion
Notes	✓ To create a proportion, simply find (or create) two equal fractions. ✓ Use cross products to solve proportions or to test whether two ratios are equal and form a proportion. $\frac{a}{b} = \frac{c}{d} \Rightarrow a \times d = c \times b$
Example	*State if this pair of ratios form a proportion.* $\frac{2}{3}$ *and* $\frac{12}{30}$ Use cross multiplication: $\frac{2}{3} = \frac{12}{30} \rightarrow 2 \times 30 = 12 \times 3 \rightarrow 60 = 36$, which is not correct. Therefore, this pair of ratios doesn't form a proportion.

Your Turn!

State if each pair of ratios form a proportion.

1) $\frac{3}{5}$ *and* $\frac{24}{45}$	2) $\frac{4}{9}$ *and* $\frac{16}{24}$
3) $\frac{3}{11}$ *and* $\frac{9}{33}$	4) $\frac{7}{10}$ *and* $\frac{14}{20}$
5) $\frac{7}{9}$ *and* $\frac{48}{81}$	6) $\frac{6}{8}$ *and* $\frac{12}{14}$
7) $\frac{2}{10}$ *and* $\frac{6}{30}$	8) $\frac{3}{18}$ *and* $\frac{19}{28}$

9) Solve.

Five pencils costs $0.50. How many pencils can you buy for $2.50? _____

Find more at

bit.ly/37GHQxp

Topic	Create Proportion – Answers
Notes	✓ To create a proportion, simply find (or create) two equal fractions. ✓ Use cross products to solve proportions or to test whether two ratios are equal and form a proportion. $\frac{a}{b} = \frac{c}{d} \Rightarrow a \times d = c \times b$
Example	*State if this pair of ratios form a proportion.* $\frac{2}{3}$ *and* $\frac{12}{30}$ Use cross multiplication: $\frac{2}{3} = \frac{12}{30} \rightarrow 2 \times 30 = 12 \times 3 \rightarrow 60 = 36$, which is not correct. Therefore, this pair of ratios doesn't form a proportion.

Your Turn!	*State if each pair of ratios form a proportion.*	
Find more at bit.ly/37GHQxp	1) $\frac{3}{5}$ and $\frac{24}{45}$, *No*	2) $\frac{4}{9}$ and $\frac{16}{24}$, *No*
	3) $\frac{3}{11}$ and $\frac{9}{33}$, *Yes*	4) $\frac{7}{10}$ and $\frac{14}{20}$, *Yes*
	5) $\frac{7}{9}$ and $\frac{48}{81}$, *No*	6) $\frac{6}{8}$ and $\frac{12}{14}$, *No*
	7) $\frac{2}{10}$ and $\frac{6}{30}$, *Yes*	8) $\frac{3}{18}$ and $\frac{19}{28}$, *No*
	9) Solve. Five pencils costs $0.50. How many pencils can you buy for $2.50? **5 pencils**	

Topic	Similarity and Ratios
Notes	✓ Two figures are similar if they have the same shape. ✓ Two or more figures are similar if the corresponding angles are equal, and the corresponding sides are in proportion.
Example	***Following triangles are similar. What is the value of unknown side?*** **Solution:** Find the corresponding sides and write a proportion: $\frac{4}{12} = \frac{x}{9}$. Now, use cross product to solve for x: $\frac{4}{12} = \frac{x}{9} \rightarrow 4 \times 9 = 12 \times x \rightarrow 36 = 12x$. Divide both sides by 12. Then: $12x = 36 \rightarrow \frac{36}{12} = \frac{12x}{12} \rightarrow x = 3$. The missing side is 3.

Your Turn!

1)

2)

3)

4)

5)

6)

Topic	Similarity and Ratios - Answers
Notes	✓ Two figures are similar if they have the same shape. ✓ Two or more figures are similar if the corresponding angles are equal, and the corresponding sides are in proportion.
Example	*Following triangles are similar. What is the value of unknown side?* **Solution:** Find the corresponding sides and write a proportion: $\frac{4}{12} = \frac{x}{9}$. Now, use cross product to solve for x: $\frac{4}{12} = \frac{x}{9} \rightarrow 4 \times 9 = 12 \times x \rightarrow 36 = 12x$. Divide both sides by 12. Then: $12x = 36 \rightarrow \frac{36}{12} = \frac{12x}{12} \rightarrow x = 3$. The missing side is 3.

Your Turn!

1) 10

2) 11

3) 4

4) 8

5) 10

6) 9

Topic	Percent Problems
Notes	✓ In each percent problem, we are looking for the base, or part or the percent. ✓ Use the following equations to find each missing section. ○ Base = Part ÷ Percent ○ Part = Percent × Base ○ Percent = Part ÷ Base
Examples	**18 *is what percent of* 30?** In this problem, we are looking for the percent. Use the following equation: $Percent = Part \div Base \rightarrow Percent = 18 \div 30 = 0.6 = 60\%$ **40 *is* 20% *of what number?*** Use the following formula: $Base = Part \div Percent \rightarrow Base = 40 \div 0.20 = 200$ 40 is 20% of 200.

Your Turn!		
	1) What is 20 percent of 500?	2) 24 is what percent of 160?
	3) 60 is 5 percent of what number?	4) 48 is what percent of 300?
	5) 84 is 28 percent of what number?	6) 63 is what percent of 700?
Find more at bit.ly/34Gy3FL	7) 63 is 21 percent of what number?	8) 42 is what percent of 600?

Topic	Percent Problems – Answers

Notes	✓ In each percent problem, we are looking for the base, or part or the percent.
	✓ Use the following equations to find each missing section.
	   ○ Base = Part ÷ Percent
	   ○ Part = Percent × Base
	   ○ Percent = Part ÷ Base

Examples	**18** *is what percent of* **30?** In this problem, we are looking for the percent. Use the following equation: $Percent = Part \div Base \rightarrow Percent = 18 \div 30 = 0.6 = 60\%$ **40** *is* **20%** *of what number?* Use the following formula: $Base = Part \div Percent \rightarrow Base = 40 \div 0.20 = 200$ 40 is 20% of 200.

Your Turn!	1) What is 20 percent of 500? 100	2) 24 is what percent of 160? 15%
	3) 60 is 5 percent of what number? 1,200	4) 48 is what percent of 300? 16%
	5) 84 is 28 percent of what number? 300	6) 63 is what percent of 700? 9%
	7) 63 is 21 percent of what number? 300	8) 42 is what percent of 600? 7%

Find more at

bit.ly/34Gy3FL

Topic	Percent of Increase and Decrease
Notes	✓ Percent of change (increase or decrease) is a mathematical concept that represents the degree of change over time. ✓ To find the percentage of increase or decrease: 　1- New Number – Original Number 　2- The result ÷ Original Number × 100 Or use this formula: Percent of change = $\dfrac{new\ number - original\ number}{original\ number} \times 100$
Example	The price of a printer increases from \$40 to \$50. What is the percent increase? **Solution:** Percent of change = $\dfrac{new\ number - original\ number}{original\ number} \times 100 =$ $\dfrac{50 - 40}{40} \times 100 = 25$ The percentage increase is 25. It means that the price of the printer increased 25%.
Your Turn!	1) In a class, the number of students has been increased from 30 to 33. What is the percentage increase? _____ % 2) The price of gasoline rose from \$4.60 to \$4.83 in one month. By what percent did the gas price rise? _____ % 3) A shirt was originally priced at \$60.00. It went on sale for \$54.00. What was the percent that the shirt was discounted? _____ % 4) Jason got a raise, and his hourly wage increased from \$40 to \$56. What is the percent increase? _____ %

Find more at

bit.ly/3pgPQes

Topic	Percent of Increase and Decrease – Answers
Notes	✓ Percent of change (increase or decrease) is a mathematical concept that represents the degree of change over time. ✓ To find the percentage of increase or decrease: 1- New Number – Original Number 2- The result ÷ Original Number × 100 Or use this formula: Percent of change $= \frac{new\ number\ -\ original\ number}{original\ number} \times 100$
Example	The price of a printer increases from \$40 to \$50. What is the percent increase? **Solution:** Percent of change $= \frac{new\ number\ -\ original\ number}{original\ number} \times 100 = \frac{50\ -\ 40}{40} \times 100 =$ 25 The percentage increase is 25. It means that the price of the printer increased 25%.
Your Turn! **Find more at** bit.ly/3pgPQes	1) In a class, the number of students has been increased from 30 to 33. What is the percentage increase? 10%
	2) The price of gasoline rose from \$4.60 to \$4.83 in one month. By what percent did the gas price rise? 5%
	3) A shirt was originally priced at \$60.00. It went on sale for \$54.00. What was the percent that the shirt was discounted? -—10%
	4) Jason got a raise, and his hourly wage increased from \$40 to \$56. What is the percent increase? 40%

Topic	Discount, Tax and Tip
Notes	✓ Discount = Multiply the regular price by the rate of discount ✓ Selling price = original price − discount ✓ To find tax, multiply the tax rate to the taxable amount (income, property value, etc.) ✓ To find tip, multiply the rate to the selling price.
Example	The original price of a table is $300 and the tax rate is 6%. What is the final price of the table? **Solution:** First find the tax amount. To find tax: Multiply the tax rate to the taxable amount. Tax rate is 6% or 0.06. Then: $0.06 \times 300 = 18$. The tax amount is $18. Final price is: $300 + $18 = $318

Your Turn!	1) Original price of a chair: $350 Tax: 12%, Selling price: _____	2) Original price of a computer: $600 Discount: 15%, Selling price: _____
	3) Original price of a printer: $250 Tax: 10%, Selling price: _____	4) Original price of a sofa: $620 Discount: 25%, Selling price: _____
	5) Original price of a mattress: $800 Tax: 12%, Selling price: _____	6) Original price of a book: $150 Discount: 60%, Selling price: _____
Find more at bit.ly/2Je5lo0	7) Restaurant bill: $24.00 Tip: 25%, Final amount: _____	8) Restaurant bill: $80.00 Tip: 15%, Final amount: _____

Topic	Discount, Tax and Tip – Answers
Notes	✓ Discount = Multiply the regular price by the rate of discount ✓ Selling price = original price – discount ✓ To find tax, multiply the tax rate to the taxable amount (income, property value, etc.) ✓ To find tip, multiply the rate to the selling price.
Example	*The original price of a table is $300 and the tax rate is 6%. What is the final price of the table?* **Solution:** First find the tax amount. To find tax: Multiply the tax rate to the taxable amount. Tax rate is 6% or 0.06. Then: $0.06 \times 300 = 18$. The tax amount is $18. Final price is: $300 + $18 = $318

Your Turn!		
	1) Original price of a chair: $350 Tax: 12%, Selling price: $392	2) Original price of a computer: $600 Discount: 15%, Selling price: $510
	3) Original price of a printer: $250 Tax: 10%, Selling price: $275	4) Original price of a sofa: $620 Discount: 25%, Selling price: $465
	5) Original price of a mattress: $800 Tax: 12%, Selling price: $896	6) Original price of a book: $150 Discount: 60%, Selling price: $60
	7) Restaurant bill: $24.00 Tip: 25%, Final amount: $30	8) Restaurant bill: $80.00 Tip: 15%, Final amount: $92

Find more at

bit.ly/2Je5lo0

Topic	Simple Interest
Notes	✓ Simple Interest: The charge for borrowing money or the return for lending it. To solve a simple interest problem, use this formula: Interest = principal x rate x time ⇒ $I = p \times r \times t$
Example	**Find simple interest for** $3,000$ **investment at** 5% **for 4 years.** **Solution:** Use Interest formula: $I = prt$ ($P = \$3{,}000$, r = $5\% = 0.05$ and $t = 4$) Then: $I = 3{,}000 \times 0.05 \times 4 = \$600$

Your Turn!		
	1) $200 at 3% for 2 years. Simple interest: $_____	2) $4,200 at 4% for 5 years. Simple interest: $_____
	3) $720 at 2% for 5 years. Simple interest: $_____	4) $2,200 at 8% for 4 years. Simple interest: $_____
	5) $1,800 at 3% for 2 years. Simple interest: $_____	6) $530 at 4% for 5 years. Simple interest: $_____
	7) $5,100 at 6% for 6 months. Simple interest: $_____	8) $960 at 5% for 3 months. Simple interest: $_____

Find more at

bit.ly/3nJli3D

Topic	Simple Interest – Answers
Notes	✓ Simple Interest: The charge for borrowing money or the return for lending it. To solve a simple interest problem, use this formula: Interest = principal x rate x time $\Rightarrow$ $I = p \times r \times t$
Example	**Find simple interest for $3,000 investment at 5% for 4 years.** **Solution:** Use Interest formula: $I = prt$ ($P = \$3,000$, r $= 5\% = 0.05$ and $t = 4$) Then: $I = 3,000 \times 0.05 \times 4 = \$600$

Your Turn!		
	1) $200 at 3% for 2 years. Simple interest: $12	2) $4,200 at 4% for 5 years. Simple interest: $840
	3) $720 at 2% for 5 years. Simple interest: $72	4) $2,200 at 8% for 4 years. Simple interest: $704
	5) $1,800 at 3% for 2 years. Simple interest: $108	6) $530 at 4% for 5 years. Simple interest: $106
Find more at bit.ly/3nJli3D	7) $5,100 at 6% for 6 months. Simple interest: $153	8) $960 at 5% for 3 months. Simple interest: $12

Topic	**Simplifying Variable Expressions**
Notes	✓ In algebra, a variable is a letter used to stand for a number. The most common letters are: $x, y, z, a, b, c, m,$ and n. ✓ Algebraic expression is an expression contains integers, variables, and the math operations such as addition, subtraction, multiplication, division, etc. ✓ In an expression, we can combine "like" terms. (values with same variable and same power)
Example	***Simplify this expression.*** $(6x + 8x + 9) = ?$ Combine like terms. Then: $(6x + 8x + 9) = 14x + 9$ **(remember you cannot combine variables and numbers).**

Your Turn!		
	1) $6x + 4 - 7x =$	2) $5 + 3x + 2x =$
	3) $8x + 3 - 3x =$	4) $-2 - x^2 - 6x^2 =$
	5) $3 + 10x^2 + 2 =$	6) $8x^2 + 6x + 7x^2 =$
	7) $5x^2 - 12x^2 + 8x =$	8) $2x^2 - 2x - x + 5x^2 =$
	9) $6x - (10 - 25x) =$	10) $16x - (60x - 50) =$

Find more at

bit.ly/2WFVudQ

Topic	Simplifying Variable Expressions – Answers
Notes	✓ In algebra, a variable is a letter used to stand for a number. The most common letters are: $x, y, z, a, b, c, m,$ and n. ✓ Algebraic expression is an expression contains integers, variables, and the math operations such as addition, subtraction, multiplication, division, etc. ✓ In an expression, we can combine "like" terms. (values with same variable and same power)
Example	*Simplify this expression*. $(6x + 8x + 9) =?$ Combine like terms. Then: $(6x + 8x + 9) = 14x + 9$ *(remember you cannot combine variables and numbers).*

Your Turn!

1) $6x + 4 - 7x =$ $\qquad -x + 4$	2) $5 + 3x + 2x =$ $\qquad 5x + 5$
3) $8x + 3 - 3x =$ $\qquad 5x + 3$	4) $-2 - x^2 - 6x^2 =$ $\qquad -7x^2 - 2$
5) $3 + 10x^2 + 2 =$ $\qquad 10x^2 + 5$	6) $8x^2 + 6x + 7x^2 =$ $\qquad 15x^2 + 6x$
7) $5x^2 - 12x^2 + 8x =$ $\qquad -7x^2 + 8x$	8) $2x^2 - 2x - x + 5x^2 =$ $\qquad 7x^2 - 3x$
9) $6x - (10 - 25x) =$ $\qquad 31x - 10$	10) $16x - (60x - 50) =$ $\qquad -44x + 50$

Find more at

bit.ly/2WFVudQ

Topic	Simplifying Polynomial Expressions
Notes	✓ In mathematics, a polynomial is an expression consisting of variables and coefficients that involves only the operations of addition, subtraction, multiplication, and non–negative integer exponents of variables. $$P(x) = a_n x^n + a_{n-1} x^{n-1} + \dots + a_2 x^2 + a_1 x + z$$
Example	*Simplify this expression.* $(2x^2 - x^4) - (4x^4 - x^2) =$ First use distributive property: → multiply $(-)$ into $(4x^4 - x^2)$ $(2x^2 - x^4) - (4x^4 - x^2) = 2x^2 - x^4 - 4x^4 + x^2$ Then combine "like" terms: $2x^2 - x^4 - 4x^4 + x^2 = 3x^2 - 5x^4$ And write in standard form: $3x^2 - 5x^4 = -5x^4 + 3x^2$

Your Turn!	1) $(x^3 + 3x^2) - (10x + 4x^2) =$	2) $(3x^5 + 5x^3) - (6x^3 + 9x^2) =$
	3) $(12x^4 + 4x^2) - (2x^2 - 6x^4) =$	4) $14x - 3x^2 - 2(6x^2 + 6x^3) =$
	5) $(5x^3 - 3) + 5(2x^2 - 3x^3) =$	6) $(4x^3 - 2x) - 2(4x^3 - 2x^4) =$
Find more at bit.ly/2WT5gtn	7) $3(3x - 2x^3) - 4(x^3 + 5x^2) =$	8) $(4x^2 - 3x) - (4x^3 + 6x^2) =$

Topic	Simplifying Polynomial Expressions – Answers
Notes	✓ In mathematics, a polynomial is an expression consisting of variables and coefficients that involves only the operations of addition, subtraction, multiplication, and non–negative integer exponents of variables. $$P(x) = a_n x^n + a_{n-1} x^{n-1} + \dots + a_2 x^2 + a_1 x + a_0$$
Example	*Simplify this expression.* $(2x^2 - x^4) - (4x^4 - x^2) =$ First use distributive property: → multiply $(-)$ into $(4x^4 - x^2)$ $(2x^2 - x^4) - (4x^4 - x^2) = 2x^2 - x^4 - 4x^4 + x^2$ Then combine "like" terms: $2x^2 - x^4 - 4x^4 + x^2 = 3x^2 - 5x^4$ And write in standard form: $3x^2 - 5x^4 = -5x^4 + 3x^2$

Your Turn!

1) $(x^3 + 3x^2) - (10x + 4x^2) =$ $x^3 - x^2 - 10x$	2) $(3x^5 + 5x^3) - (6x^3 + 9x^2) =$ $3x^5 - x^3 - 9x^2$
3) $(12x^4 + 4x^2) - (2x^2 - 6x^4) =$ $18x^4 + 2x^2$	4) $14x - 3x^2 - 2(6x^2 + 6x^3) =$ $-12x^3 - 15x^2 + 14x$
5) $(5x^3 - 3) + 5(2x^2 - 3x^3) =$ $-10x^3 + 10x^2 - 3$	6) $(4x^3 - 2x) - 2(4x^3 - 2x^4) =$ $4x^4 - 4x^3 - 2x$
7) $3(3x - 2x^3) - 4(x^3 + 5x^2) =$ $-10x^3 - 20x^2 + 9x$	8) $(4x^2 - 3x) - (4x^3 + 6x^2) =$ $-4x^3 - 2x^2 - 3x$

Find more at

bit.ly/2WT5gtn

Topic	**Evaluating One Variable**
Notes	✓ To evaluate one variable expression, find the variable and substitute a number for that variable. ✓ Perform the arithmetic operations.
Example	***Find the value of this expression for*** $x = -3$. $\quad -3x - 13$ **Solution:** Substitute -3 for x, then: $-3x - 13 = -3(-3) - 13 = 9 - 13 = -4$

Your Turn!	1) $x = -2 \Rightarrow 4x + 9 =$ ____	2) $x = 3 \Rightarrow 5(3x + 5) =$ ____
	3) $x = -1 \Rightarrow 6x + 4 =$ ____	4) $x = 7 \Rightarrow 6(5x + 3) =$ ____
	5) $x = 4 \Rightarrow 5(3x + 2) =$ ____	6) $x = 6 \Rightarrow 3(2x + 4) =$ ____
	7) $x = 3 \Rightarrow 7(3x + 1) =$ ____	8) $x = 8 \Rightarrow 3(3x + 7) =$ ____
Find more at bit.ly/3ppujQZ	9) $x = 8 \Rightarrow 3(x + 6) =$ ____	10) $x = 6 \Rightarrow 3(2x + 3) =$ ____

Topic	Evaluating One Variable – Answers
Notes	✓ To evaluate one variable expression, find the variable and substitute a number for that variable. ✓ Perform the arithmetic operations.
Example	*Find the value of this expression for* $x = -3$. $\quad -3x - 13$ **Solution:** Substitute -3 for x, then: $-3x - 13 = -3(-3) - 13 = 9 - 13 = -4$

Your Turn!		
	1) $x = -2 \Rightarrow 4x + 9 = 1$	2) $x = 3 \Rightarrow 5(3x + 5) = 70$
	3) $x = -1 \Rightarrow 6x + 4 = -2$	4) $x = 7 \Rightarrow 6(5x + 3) = 228$
	5) $x = 4 \Rightarrow 5(3x + 2) = 70$	6) $x = 6 \Rightarrow 3(2x + 4) = 48$
	7) $x = 3 \Rightarrow 7(3x + 1) = 70$	8) $x = 8 \Rightarrow 3(3x + 7) = 93$
Find more at bit.ly/3ppujQZ	9) $x = 8 \Rightarrow 3(x + 6) = 42$	10) $x = 6 \Rightarrow 3(2x + 3) = 45$

Topic	**Evaluating Two Variables**
Notes	✓ To evaluate an algebraic expression, substitute a number for each variable. ✓ Perform the arithmetic operations to find the value of the expression.
Example	**Evaluate this expression for** $a = 4$ **and** $b = -2$. $\quad 5a - 6b$ **Solution:** Substitute 4 for a, and -2 for b, then: $5a - 6b = \ 5(4) - 6(-2) = 20 + 12 = 32$

Your Turn!

1) $-3a + 5b$, $a = 3$, $b = 2$ _____	2) $4x + 2y$, $x = -1$, $y = 4$ _____
3) $-5a + 3b$, $a = 2$, $b = -2$ _____	4) $3x - 4y$, $x = 6$, $y = 2$ _____
5) $2z + 14 + 6k$, $z = 5$, $k = 3$ _____	6) $7a - (9 - 3b)$, $a = 1$, $b = 1$ _____
7) $-6a + 3b$, $a = 4$, $b = 3$ _____	8) $-2a + b$, $a = 6$, $b = 9$ _____
9) $5x + 3y$, $x = 2$, $y = 9$ _____	10) $z + 7 + 3k$, $z = 4$, $k = 2$ _____

Find more at

bit.ly/2JfrzWJ

Topic	**Evaluating Two Variables – Answers**
Notes	✓ To evaluate an algebraic expression, substitute a number for each variable. ✓ Perform the arithmetic operations to find the value of the expression.
Example	**Evaluate this expression for** $a = 4$ **and** $b = -2$. $5a - 6b$ **Solution:** Substitute 4 for a, and -2 for b, then: $5a - 6b = 5(4) - 6(-2) = 20 + 12 = 32$

Your Turn!

1) $-3a + 5b,\ a = 3,\ b = 2$ 1	2) $4x + 2y,\ x = -1,\ y = 4$ 4
3) $-5a + 3b,\ a = 2,\ b = -2$ -16	4) $3x - 4y,\ x = 6,\ y = 2$ 10
5) $2z + 14 + 6k,\ z = 5,\ k = 3$ 42	6) $7a - (9 - 3b),\ a = 1,\ b = 1$ 1
7) $-6a + 3b,\ a = 4,\ b = 3$ -15	8) $-2a + b,\ a = 6,\ b = 9$ -3
9) $5x + 3y,\ x = 2,\ y = 9$ 37	10) $z + 7 + 3k,\ z = 4,\ k = 2$ 17

Find more at

bit.ly/2JfrzWJ

Topic	The Distributive Property
Notes	✓ The distributive property (or the distributive property of multiplication over addition and subtraction) simplifies and solves expressions in the form of: $a(b + c)$ or $a(b - c)$ ✓ Distributive Property rule: $$a(b + c) = ab + ac$$
Example	***Simply***. $(5)(2x - 8)$ **Solution:** Use Distributive Property rule: $a(b + c) = ab + ac$ $$(5)(2x - 8) = (5 \times 2x) + (5) \times (-8) = 10x - 40$$

Your Turn!		
Find more at bit.ly/38qCaXs	1) $(-3)(2 - 4x) =$	2) $(3 - 2x)(-5)$
	3) $6\,(5 - 9x) =$	4) $10(3 - 5x) =$
	5) $5(6 - 5x) =$	6) $(-2)(-5x + 3) =$
	7) $(8 - 9x)(5) =$	8) $(-16x + 15)(-3) =$
	9) $(-6x + 8)(4) =$	10) $(-12x + 21)(-3) =$

Topic	The Distributive Property – Answers
Notes	✓ The distributive property (or the distributive property of multiplication over addition and subtraction) simplifies and solves expressions in the form of: $a(b + c)$ or $a(b - c)$ ✓ Distributive Property rule: $$a(b + c) = ab + ac$$
Example	**Simply.** $(5)(2x - 8)$ **Solution:** Use Distributive Property rule: $a(b + c) = ab + ac$ $$(5)(2x - 8) = (5 \times 2x) + (5) \times (-8) = 10x - 40$$

Your Turn!		
	1) $(-3)(2 - 4x) = 12x - 6$	2) $(3 - 2x)(-5) = 10x - 15$
	3) $6(5 - 9x) = -54x + 30$	4) $10(3 - 5x) = -50x + 30$
	5) $5(6 - 5x) = -25x + 30$	6) $(-2)(-5x + 3) = 10x - 6$
	7) $(8 - 9x)(5) = -45x + 40$	8) $(-16x + 15)(-3) =$ $48x - 45$
Find more at bit.ly/38qCaXs	9) $(-6x + 8)(4) = -24x + 32$	10) $(-12x + 21)(-3) =$ $36x - 63$

Topic	One–Step Equations

Notes	✓ You only need to perform one Math operation in order to solve the one-step equations.
	
	✓ To solve one-step equation, find the inverse (opposite) operation is being performed.
	
	✓ The inverse operations are:
	
	    - Addition and subtraction
	
	    - Multiplication and division

Example	***Solve this equation.*** $x + 42 = 60 \Rightarrow x = ?$ Here, the operation is addition and its inverse operation is subtraction. To solve this equation, subtract 42 from both sides of the *equation:* $x + 42 - 42 = 60 - 42$ Then simplify: $x + 42 - 42 = 60 - 42 \Rightarrow x = 18$

Your Turn!	1) $x - 12 = 44 \Rightarrow x = \underline{\quad}$	2) $15 = 11 + x \Rightarrow x = \underline{\quad}$
	3) $x - 22 = 54 \Rightarrow x = \underline{\quad}$	4) $x + 14 = 24 \Rightarrow x = \underline{\quad}$
Find more at bit.ly/37Jq0tK	5) $4x = 24 \Rightarrow x = \underline{\quad}$	6) $\frac{x}{6} = -3 \Rightarrow x = \underline{\quad}$
	7) $66 = 22x \Rightarrow x = \underline{\quad}$	8) $\frac{x}{18} = 3 \Rightarrow x = \underline{\quad}$

Topic	One–Step Equations – Answers
Notes	✓ You only need to perform one Math operation in order to solve the one-step equations. ✓ To solve one-step equation, find the inverse (opposite) operation is being performed. ✓ The inverse operations are: - Addition and subtraction - Multiplication and division
Example	*Solve this equation*. $x + 42 = 60 \Rightarrow x = ?$ Here, the operation is addition and its inverse operation is subtraction. To solve this equation, subtract 42 from both sides of the *equation:* $x + 42 - 42 = 60 - 42$ Then simplify: $x + 42 - 42 = 60 - 42 \Rightarrow x = 18$

Your Turn!	1) $x - 12 = 44 \Rightarrow x = 56$	2) $15 = 11 + x \Rightarrow x = 4$
	3) $x - 22 = 54 \Rightarrow x = 76$	4) $x + 14 = 24 \Rightarrow x = 10$
	5) $4x = 24 \Rightarrow x = 6$	6) $\frac{x}{6} = -3 \Rightarrow x = -18$
Find more at bit.ly/37Jq0tK	7) $66 = 22x \Rightarrow x = 3$	8) $\frac{x}{18} = 3 \Rightarrow x = 54$

Topic	Multi –Step Equations
Notes	✓ Combine "like" terms on one side. ✓ Bring variables to one side by adding or subtracting. ✓ Simplify using the inverse of addition or subtraction. ✓ Simplify further by using the inverse of multiplication or division. ✓ Check your solution by plugging the value of the variable into the original equation.
Example	*Solve this equation for* x. $2x - 3 = 13$ **Solution:** The inverse of subtraction is addition. Add 3 to both sides of the equation. Then: $2x - 3 = 13 \Rightarrow 2x - 3 = 13 + 3$ $\Rightarrow 2x = 16$. Now, divide both sides by 2, then: $\frac{2x}{2} = \frac{16}{2} \Rightarrow x = 8$ Now, check the solution: $x = 8 \Rightarrow 2x - 3 = 13 \Rightarrow 2(8) - 3 = 13 \Rightarrow 16 - 3 = 13$ The answer $x = 8$ is correct.

Your Turn!	1) $5x - 15 = 10 \Rightarrow x =$	2) $14 - 2x = -6 + 2x \Rightarrow x =$
	3) $3(4 - 2x) = 24 \Rightarrow x =$	4) $15 + 5x = -7 - 6x \Rightarrow x =$
Find more at bit.ly/3nQbSEB	5) $-2(5 + x) = 2 \Rightarrow x =$	6) $12 - 2x = -3 - 5x \Rightarrow x =$
	7) $18 = -(x - 8) \Rightarrow x =$	8) $13 - 5x = -5 - 2x \Rightarrow x =$

Topic	Multi –Step Equations – Answers
Notes	✓ Combine "like" terms on one side. ✓ Bring variables to one side by adding or subtracting. ✓ Simplify using the inverse of addition or subtraction. ✓ Simplify further by using the inverse of multiplication or division. ✓ Check your solution by plugging the value of the variable into the original equation.
Example	*Solve this equation for* x. $2\text{x} - 3 = 13$ **Solution:** The inverse of subtraction is addition. Add 3 to both sides of the equation. Then: $2\text{x} - 3 = 13 \Rightarrow 2\text{x} - 3 = 13 + 3$ $\Rightarrow 2\text{x} = 16$. Now, divide both sides by 2, then: $\frac{2x}{2} = \frac{16}{2} \Rightarrow \text{x} = 8$ Now, check the solution: $x = 8 \Rightarrow 2\text{x} - 3 = 13 \Rightarrow 2(8) - 3 = 13 \Rightarrow 16 - 3 = 13$ The answer $x = 8$ is correct.

Your Turn!		
	1) $5x - 15 = 10 \Rightarrow x = 5$	2) $14 - 2x = -6 + 2x \Rightarrow x = 5$
	3) $3(4 - 2x) = 24 \Rightarrow x = -2$	4) $15 + 5x = -7 - 6x \Rightarrow x = -2$
	5) $-2(5 + x) = 2 \Rightarrow x = -6$	6) $12 - 2x = -3 - 5x \Rightarrow x = -5$
	7) $18 = -(x - 8) \Rightarrow x = -10$	8) $13 - 5x = -5 - 2x \Rightarrow x = 6$

Find more at

bit.ly/3nObSFB

Topic	System of Equations
Notes	✓ A system of equations contains two equations and two variables. For example, consider the system of equations: $x - 2y = -2, x + 2y = 10$ ✓ The easiest way to solve a system of equation is using the elimination method. The elimination method uses the addition property of equality. You can add the same value to each side of an equation. ✓ For the first equation above, you can add $x + 2y$ to the left side and 10 to the right side of the first equation: $x - 2y + (x + 2y) = -2 + 10$. Now, if you simplify, you get: $x - 2y + (x + 2y) = -2 + 10 \rightarrow 2x = 8 \rightarrow x = 4$. Now, substitute 4 for the x in the first equation: $4 - 2y = -2$. By solving this equation, $y = 3$
Example	What is the value of x and y in this system of equations? $\begin{cases} 3x - y = 7 \\ -x + 4y = 5 \end{cases}$ **Solution:** Solving System of Equations by Elimination: $\begin{array}{r} 3x - y = 7 \\ -x + 4y = 5 \\ \hline \end{array}$ Multiply the second equation by 3, then add it to the first equation. $\begin{array}{r} 3x - y = 7 \\ 3(-x + 4y = 5) \end{array} \Rightarrow \begin{array}{r} 3x - y = 7 \\ -3x + 12y = 15 \end{array} \Rightarrow 11y = 22 \Rightarrow y = 2$. Now, substitute 2 for y in the first equation and solve for x. $3x - (2) = 7 \Rightarrow 3x = 9 \Rightarrow x = 3$
Your Turn! **Find more at** bit.ly/3mPGO6k	1) $-4x + 4y = 8$ $\qquad -4x + 2y = 6$ $x = $ ___ $y = $ ___ 2) $-5x + y = -3$ $\qquad 3x - 8y = 24$ $x = $ ___ $y = $ ___ 3) $y = -2$ $\qquad 4x - 3y = 8$ $x = $ ___ $y = $ ___ 4) $y = -3x + 5$ $\qquad 5x - 4y = -3$ $x = $ ___ $y = $ ___ 5) $20x - 18y = -26$ $\qquad -10x + 6y = 22$ $x = $ ___ $y = $ ___ 6) $-9x - 12y = 15$ $\qquad 2x - 6y = 14$ $x = $ ___ $\qquad y = $ ___

Topic	System of Equations- Answers
Notes	✓ A system of equations contains two equations and two variables. For example, consider the system of equations: $x - 2y = -2, x + 2y = 10$ ✓ The easiest way to solve a system of equation is using the elimination method. The elimination method uses the addition property of equality. You can add the same value to each side of an equation. ✓ For the first equation above, you can add $x + 2y$ to the left side and 10 to the right side of the first equation: $x - 2y + (x + 2y) = -2 + 10$. Now, if you simplify, you get: $x - 2y + (x + 2y) = -2 + 10 \rightarrow 2x = 8 \rightarrow x = 4$. Now, substitute 4 for the x in the first equation: $4 - 2y = -2$. By solving this equation, $y = 3$
Example	What is the value of x and y in this system of equations? $\begin{cases} 3x - y = 7 \\ -x + 4y = 5 \end{cases}$ **Solution:** Solving System of Equations by Elimination: $\begin{array}{c} 3x - y = 7 \\ -x + 4y = 5 \\ \hline \end{array}$ Multiply the second equation by 3, then add it to the first equation. $\begin{array}{c} 3x - y = 7 \\ 3(-x + 4y = 5) \\ \hline \end{array} \Rightarrow \begin{array}{c} 3x - y = 7 \\ -3x + 12y = 15) \\ \hline \end{array} \Rightarrow 11y = 22 \Rightarrow y = 2$. Now, substitute 2 for y in the first equation and solve for x. $3x - (2) = 7 \Rightarrow 3x = 9 \Rightarrow x = 3$

Your Turn!	1) $-4x + 4y = 8$ $ -4x + 2y = 6$ $ x = -1$ $ y = 1$	2) $-5x + y = -3$ $ 3x - 8y = 24$ $ x = 0$ $ y = -3$
	3) $y = -2$ $ 4x - 3y = 8$ $ x = \dfrac{1}{2}$ $ y = -2$	4) $y = -3x + 5$ $ 5x - 4y = -3$ $ x = 1$ $ y = 2$
Find more at bit.ly/3mPGO6k	5) $20x - 18y = -26$ $ -10x + 6y = 22$ $ x = -4$ $ y = -3$	6) $-9x - 12y = 15$ $ 2x - 6y = 14$ $ x = 1$ $ y = -2$

Topic	Graphing Single–Variable Inequalities
Notes	✓ An inequality compares two expressions using an inequality sign. ✓ Inequality signs are: “less than" $<$, "greater than" $>$, “less than or equal to” $\leq$, and “greater than or equal to” $\geq$. ✓ To graph a single–variable inequality, find the value of the inequality on the number line. ✓ For less than ($<$) or greater than ($>$) draw open circle on the value of the variable. If there is an equal sign too, then use filled circle. ✓ Draw an arrow to the right for greater or to the left for less than.
Example	***Draw a graph for this inequality.*** $x < 5$ **Solution:** Since, the variable is less than 5, then we need to find 5 in the number line and draw an open circle on it. Then, draw an arrow to the left. 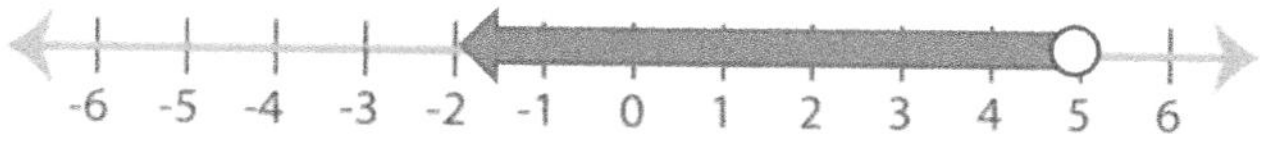

Your Turn!

1) $x < 3$

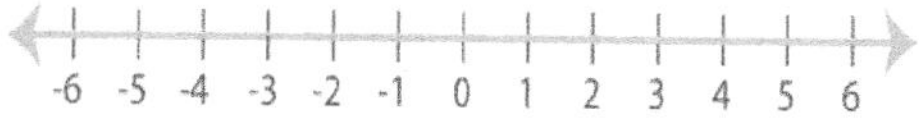

2) $x \geq -2$

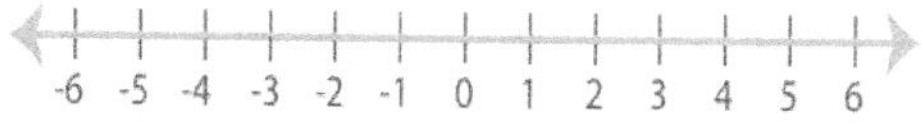

3) $x \geq -3$

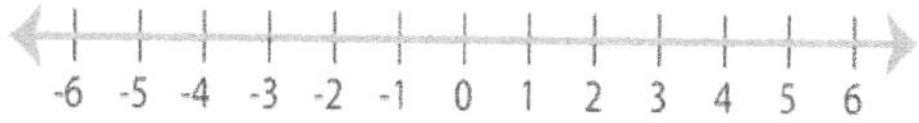

4) $x \leq 6$

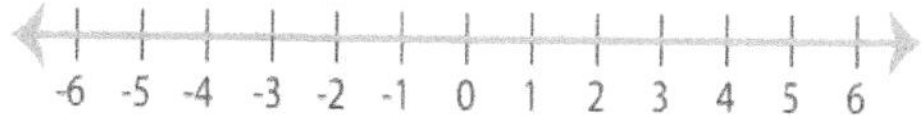

5) $x > -6$

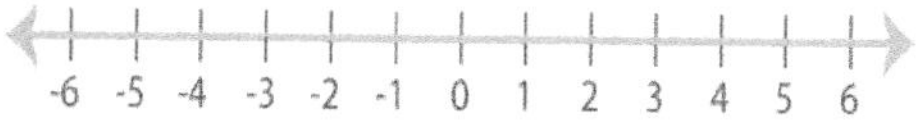

6) $2 > x$

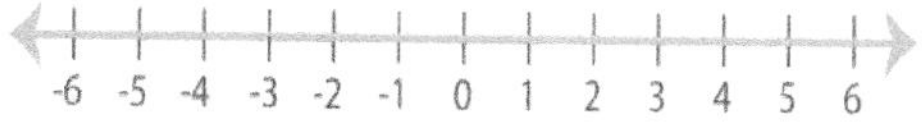

7) $-3 \leq x$

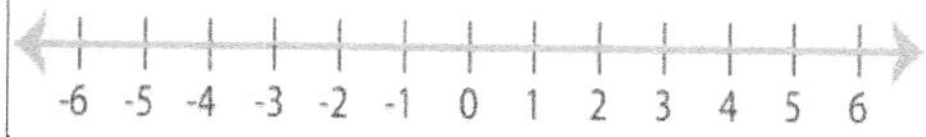

8) $x > 1$

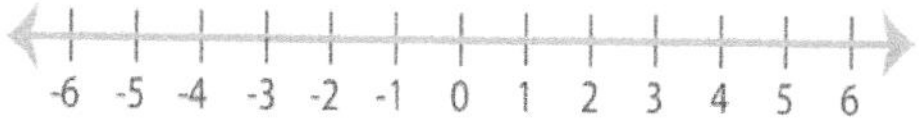

Find more at

bit.ly/3aJ4GGo

Topic	Graphing Single–Variable Inequalities- Answers
Notes	✓ An inequality compares two expressions using an inequality sign. ✓ Inequality signs are: "less than" <, "greater than" >, "less than or equal to" ≤, and "greater than or equal to" ≥. ✓ To graph a single–variable inequality, find the value of the inequality on the number line. ✓ For less than (<) or greater than (>) draw open circle on the value of the variable. If there is an equal sign too, then use filled circle. ✓ Draw an arrow to the right for greater or to the left for less than.
Example	***Draw a graph for this inequality.*** $x < 5$ **Solution:** Since, the variable is less than 5, then we need to find 5 in the number line and draw an open circle on it. Then, draw an arrow to the left.

Your Turn!	1) $x < 3$ 	2) $x \geq -2$
	3) $x \geq -3$ 	4) $x \leq 6$
Find more at bit.ly/3aJ4GGo 	5) $x > -6$ 	6) $2 > x$
	7) $-3 \leq x$ 	8) $x > 1$

Topic	One–Step Inequalities
Notes	✓ Inequality signs are: "less than" $<$, "greater than" $>$, "less than or equal to" $\leq$, and "greater than or equal to" $\geq$. ✓ You only need to perform one Math operation in order to solve the one-step inequalities. ✓ To solve one-step inequalities, find the inverse (opposite) operation is being performed. ✓ For dividing or multiplying both sides by negative numbers, flip the direction of the inequality sign.
Example	***Solve this inequality.*** $x + 12 < 60 \Rightarrow$ _____ Here, the operation is addition and its inverse operation is subtraction. To solve this inequality, subtract 12 from both sides of the ***inequality:*** $x + 12 - 12 < 60 - 12$ Then simplify: $x < 48$
Your Turn!	1) $3x < -9 \Rightarrow$ _____ 2) $x + 5 > 29 \Rightarrow$ _____ 3) $-3x \geq 36 \Rightarrow$ _____ 4) $x - 16 \leq 4 \Rightarrow$ _____ 5) $\frac{x}{2} \geq -9 \Rightarrow$ _____ 6) $48 < 6x \Rightarrow$ _____ 7) $88 \leq 22x \Rightarrow$ _____ 8) $\frac{x}{6} > 8 \Rightarrow$ _____

Find more at

bit.ly/3rrElgL

Topic	One–Step Inequalities - Answers
Notes	✓ Inequality signs are: "less than" <, "greater than" >, "less than or equal to" ≤, and "greater than or equal to" ≥. ✓ You only need to perform one Math operation in order to solve the one-step inequalities. ✓ To solve one-step inequalities, find the inverse (opposite) operation is being performed. ✓ For dividing or multiplying both sides by negative numbers, flip the direction of the inequality sign.
Example	***Solve this inequality.*** $\ x + 12 < 60 \Rightarrow$ _____ Here, the operation is addition and its inverse operation is subtraction. To solve this inequality, subtract 12 from both sides of the ***inequality:*** $x + 12 - 12 < 60 - 12$ Then simplify: $x < 48$

Your Turn!		
	1) $3x < -9 \Rightarrow x < -3$	2) $x + 5 > 29 \Rightarrow x > 24$
	3) $-3x \geq 36 \Rightarrow x \leq -12$	4) $x - 16 \leq 4 \Rightarrow x \leq 20$
	5) $\frac{x}{2} \geq -9 \Rightarrow x \geq -18$	6) $48 < 6x \Rightarrow 8 < x$
Find more at bit.ly/3rrElgL	7) $88 \leq 22x \Rightarrow 4 \leq x$	8) $\frac{x}{6} > 8 \Rightarrow x > 48$

Topic	**Multi –Step Inequalities**
Notes	✓ Isolate the variable. ✓ Simplify using the inverse of addition or subtraction. ✓ Simplify further by using the inverse of multiplication or division. ✓ For dividing or multiplying both sides by negative numbers, flip the direction of the inequality sign.
Example	***Solve this inequality.*** $3x + 12 \leq 21$ **Solution:** First subtract 12 from both sides: $3x + 12 - 12 \leq 21 - 12$ Then simplify: $3x + 12 - 12 \leq 21 - 12 \rightarrow 3x \leq 9$ Now divide both sides by 3: $\frac{3x}{3} \leq \frac{9}{3} \rightarrow x \leq 3$

Your Turn!	1) $4x + 3 < 39 \rightarrow$ _____	2) $5x - 9 \leq 6 \rightarrow$ _____
	3) $2x - 5 \leq 17 \rightarrow$ _____	4) $14 - 7x \geq -7 \rightarrow$ _____
	5) $18 - 6x \geq -6 \rightarrow$ _____	6) $2x - 18 \leq 16 \rightarrow$ _____
Find more at bit.ly/2WK1xOr	7) $9 + 6x < 45 \rightarrow$ _____	8) $7 - 4x < 19 \rightarrow$ _____

Topic	Multi –Step Inequalities – Answers
Notes	✓ Isolate the variable. ✓ Simplify using the inverse of addition or subtraction. ✓ Simplify further by using the inverse of multiplication or division. ✓ For dividing or multiplying both sides by negative numbers, flip the direction of the inequality sign.
Example	*Solve this inequality.* $3x + 12 \leq 21$ **Solution:** First subtract 12 from both sides: $3x + 12 - 12 \leq 21 - 12$ Then simplify: $3x + 12 - 12 \leq 21 - 12 \rightarrow 3x \leq 9$ Now divide both sides by 3: $\frac{3x}{3} \leq \frac{9}{3} \rightarrow x \leq 3$

Your Turn!	1) $4x + 3 < 39 \rightarrow x < 9$	2) $5x - 9 \leq 6 \rightarrow x \leq 3$
	3) $2x - 5 \leq 17 \rightarrow x \leq 11$	4) $14 - 7x \geq -7 \rightarrow x \leq 3$
	5) $18 - 6x \geq -6 \rightarrow x \leq 4$	6) $2x - 18 \leq 16 \rightarrow x \leq 17$
Find more at bit.ly/2WK1xOr	7) $9 + 6x < 45 \rightarrow x < 6$	8) $7 - 4x < 19 \rightarrow x > -3$

Topic	**Finding Slope**
Notes	✓ The slope of a line represents the direction of a line on the coordinate plane. ✓ A line on coordinate plane can be drawn by connecting two points. ✓ To find the slope of a line, we need two points. ✓ The slope of a line with two points A (x_1, y_1) and B (x_2, y_2) can be found by using this formula: $\frac{y_2 - y_1}{x_2 - x_1} = \frac{rise}{run}$ ✓ The equation of a line is typically written as $y = mx + b$ where m is the slope and b is the y-intercept.
Examples	***Find the slope of the line through these two points:*** $(4, -12)$ *and* $(9, 8)$. **Solution:** Slope $= \frac{y_2 - y_1}{x_2 - x_1}$. Let (x_1, y_1) be $(4, -12)$ and (x_2, y_2) be $(9, 8)$. ***Then:*** slope $= \frac{y_2 - y_1}{x_2 - x_1} = \frac{8 - (-12)}{9 - 4} = \frac{8 + 12}{5} = \frac{20}{5} = 4$ ***Find the slope of the line with equation*** $y = 5x - 6$ **Solution:** when the equation of a line is written in the form of $y = mx + b$, the slope is m. In this line: $y = 5x - 6$, the slope is 5.
Your Turn! **Find more at** bit.ly/3nMJYJv	1) $(1, 3), (5, 7)$ Slope = ____ 2) $(-2, 2), (0, 4)$ Slope = ____ 3) $(4, -2), (2, 4)$ Slope = ____ 4) $(-4, -1), (0, 7)$ Slope = ____ 5) $y = 4x + 15$ Slope = ____ 6) $y = -6x + 3$ Slope = ____

Topic	Finding Slope – Answers
Notes	✓ The slope of a line represents the direction of a line on the coordinate plane. ✓ A line on coordinate plane can be drawn by connecting two points. ✓ To find the slope of a line, we need two points. ✓ The slope of a line with two points A (x_1, y_1) and B (x_2, y_2) can be found by using this formula: $\frac{y_2 - y_1}{x_2 - x_1} = \frac{rise}{run}$ ✓ The equation of a line is typically written as $y = mx + b$ where m is the slope and b is the y-intercept.
Examples	***Find the slope of the line through these two points:*** $(4, -12)$ *and* $(9, 8)$. **Solution:** Slope $= \frac{y_2 - y_1}{x_2 - x_1}$. Let (x_1, y_1) be $(4, -12)$ and (x_2, y_2) be $(9, 8)$. ***Then:*** slope $= \frac{y_2 - y_1}{x_2 - x_1} = \frac{8 - (-12)}{9 - 4} = \frac{8 + 12}{5} = \frac{20}{5} = 4$ ***Find the slope of the line with equation*** $y = 5x - 6$ **Solution:** when the equation of a line is written in the form of $y = mx + b$, the slope is m. In this line: $y = 5x - 6$, the slope is 5.

Your Turn!	1) $(1, 3), (5, 7)$ Slope $= 1$	2) $(-2, 2), (0, 4)$ Slope $= 1$
	3) $(4, -2), (2, 4)$ Slope $= -3$	4) $(-4, -1), (0, 7)$ Slope $= 2$
Find more at bit.ly/3nMJYJv	5) $y = 4x + 15$ Slope $= 4$	6) $y = 6x + 3$ Slope $= 6$

Topic	**Graphing Lines Using Slope–Intercept Form**
Notes	✓ Slope–intercept form of a line: given the slope m and the y–intercept (the intersection of the line and y-axis) b, then the equation of the line is: $$y = mx + b$$
Example	***Sketch the graph of*** $y = -2\text{x} - 1$. **Solution:** To graph this line, we need to find two points. When x is zero the value of y is -1. And when y is zero the value of x is $-\frac{1}{2}$. $$x = 0 \rightarrow y = -2(0) - 1 = -1, y = 0 \rightarrow 0$$ $$= -2x - 1 \rightarrow x = -\frac{1}{2}$$ Now, we have two points: $(0, -1)$ and $(-\frac{1}{2}, 0)$. Find the points and graph the line. Remember that the slope of the line is $-\frac{1}{2}$.
Your Turn! **Find more at** bit.ly/3hfdnJL	1) $y = -4x + 1$ 2) $y = -x - 5$

Topic	Graphing Lines Using Slope–Intercept Form - Answers
Notes	✓ Slope–intercept form of a line: given the slope m and the y–intercept (the intersection of the line and y-axis) b, then the equation of the line is: $$y = mx + b$$
Example	***Sketch the graph of*** $y = -2x - 1.$ **Solution:** To graph this line, we need to find two points. When x is zero the value of y is -1. And when y is zero the value of x is $-\frac{1}{2}$. $x = 0 \rightarrow y = -2(0) - 1 = -1, y = 0 \rightarrow 0$ $\qquad = -2x - 1 \rightarrow x = -\frac{1}{2}$ Now, we have two points: $(0, -1)$ and $(-\frac{1}{2}, 0)$. Find the points and graph the line. Remember that the slope of the line is $-\frac{1}{2}$.
Your Turn! **Find more at** bit.ly/3hfdnJL 	1) $y = -4x + 1$ 2) $y = -x - 5$

Topic	Writing Linear Equations
Notes	✓ The equation of a line: $y = mx + b$ ✓ Identify the slope. ✓ Find the y–intercept. This can be done by substituting the slope and the coordinates of a point (x, y) on the line.
Example	**Write the equation of the line through** $(3, 1)$ **and** $(-1, 5)$. **Solution:** $Slop = \frac{y_2 - y_1}{x_2 - x_1} = \frac{5-1}{-1-3} = \frac{4}{-4} = -1 \rightarrow m = -1$ To find the value of b, you can use either points. The answer will be the same: $y = -x + b$ $(3, 1) \rightarrow 1 = -3 + b \rightarrow b = 4$ $(-1, 5) \rightarrow 5 = -(-1) + b \rightarrow b = 4$ The equation of the line is: $y = -x + 4$

Your Turn!

1) through: $(-1, 2), (1, 4)$

$y =$

2) through: $(8, 1), (5, 4)$

$y =$

3) through: $(5, -1), (8, 2)$

$y =$

4) through: $(-2, 4), (4, -8)$

$y =$

5) through: $(6, -5), (-5, 6)$

$y =$

6) through: $(4, -4), (-2, 8)$

$y =$

7) through $(-3, 6)$, Slope: 2

$y =$

8) through $(4, 3)$, Slope: -4

$y =$

Find more at
bit.ly/3nMKcAl

Topic	Writing Linear Equations – Answers
Notes	✓ The equation of a line: $y = mx + b$ ✓ Identify the slope. ✓ Find the y–intercept. This can be done by substituting the slope and the coordinates of a point (x, y) on the line.
Example	**Write the equation of the line through $(3, 1)$ and $(-1, 5)$.** **Solution:** $Slop = \frac{y_2 - y_1}{x_2 - x_1} = \frac{5 - 1}{-1 - 3} = \frac{4}{-4} = -1 \rightarrow m = -1$ To find the value of b, you can use either points. The answer will be the same: $y = -x + b$ $(3, 1) \rightarrow 1 = -3 + b \rightarrow b = 4$ $(-1, 5) \rightarrow 5 = -(-1) + b \rightarrow b = 4$ The equation of the line is: $y = -x + 4$

Your Turn!		
	1) through: $(-1, 2), (1, 4)$ $y = x + 3$	2) through: $(8, 1), (5, 4)$ $y = -x + 9$
	3) through: $(5, -1), (8, 2)$ $y = x - 6$	4) through: $(-2, 4), (4, -8)$ $y = -2x$
	5) through: $(6, -5), (-5, 6)$ $y = -x + 1$	6) through: $(4, -4), (-2, 8)$ $y = -2x + 4$
Find more at bit.ly/3nMKcAl	7) through $(-3, 6)$, Slope: 2 $y = 2x + 12$	8) through $(4, 3)$, Slope: -4 $y = -4x + 19$

Topic	**Finding Midpoint**
Notes	✓ The middle of a line segment is its midpoint. ✓ The Midpoint of two endpoints A (x_1, y_1) and B (x_2, y_2) can be found using this formula: $M(\frac{x_1+x_2}{2}, \frac{y_1+y_2}{2})$
Example	Find the midpoint of the line segment with the given endpoints. $(\mathbf{1}, -\mathbf{2}), (\mathbf{3}, \mathbf{6})$ **Solution:** Midpoint $= (\frac{x_1+x_2}{2}, \frac{y_1+y_2}{2}) \rightarrow (x_1, y_1) = (1, -2)$ and $(x_2, y_2) = (3, 6)$ Midpoint $= (\frac{1+3}{2}, \frac{-2+6}{2}) \rightarrow (\frac{4}{2}, \frac{4}{2}) \rightarrow M(2, 2)$

Your Turn!	
1) $(2, 1), (-4, 1)$ **Midpoint** $= (\_\_, \_\_)$	2) $(6, -2), (2, 4)$ **Midpoint** $= (\_\_, \_\_)$
3) $(-3, 4), (-5, 0)$ **Midpoint** $= (\_\_, \_\_)$	4) $(8, 1), (-4, 5)$ **Midpoint** $= (\_\_, \_\_)$
5) $(6, 7), (-4, 5)$ **Midpoint** $= (\_\_, \_\_)$	6) $(2, -3), (2, 5)$ **Midpoint** $= (\_\_, \_\_)$
7) $(7, 3), (-1, -7)$ **Midpoint** $= (\_\_, \_\_)$	8) $(3, 9), (-1, 5)$ **Midpoint** $= (\_\_, \_\_)$
9) $(5, 2), (-9, 0)$ **Midpoint** $= (\_\_, \_\_)$	10) $(2, 7), (10, -9)$ **Midpoint** $= (\_\_, \_\_)$

Find more at

bit.ly/3nPdnTq

Topic	Finding Midpoint – Answers
Notes	✓ The middle of a line segment is its midpoint. ✓ The Midpoint of two endpoints A (x_1, y_1) and B (x_2, y_2) can be found using this formula: $M(\frac{x_1+x_2}{2}, \frac{y_1+y_2}{2})$
Example	Find the midpoint of the line segment with the given endpoints. $(1, -2), (3, 6)$ **Solution:** Midpoint $= (\frac{x_1+x_2}{2}, \frac{y_1+y_2}{2}) \rightarrow (x_1, y_1) = (1, -2)$ and $(x_2, y_2) = (3, 6)$ Midpoint $= (\frac{1+3}{2}, \frac{-2+6}{2}) \rightarrow (\frac{4}{2}, \frac{4}{2}) \rightarrow M(2, 2)$

Your Turn!	1) $(2, 1), (-4, 1)$ **Midpoint** $= (-1, 1)$	2) $(6, -2), (2, 4)$ **Midpoint** $= (4, 1)$
	3) $(-3, 4), (-5, 0)$ **Midpoint** $= (-4, 2)$	4) $(8, 1), (-4, 5)$ **Midpoint** $= (2, 3)$
	5) $(6, 7), (-4, 5)$ **Midpoint** $= (1, 6)$	6) $(2, -3), (2, 5)$ **Midpoint** $= (2, 1)$
	7) $(7, 3), (-1, -7)$ **Midpoint** $= (3, -2)$	8) $(3, 9), (-1, 5)$ **Midpoint** $= (1, 7)$
Find more at bit.ly/3nPdnTq	9) $(5, 2), (-9, 0)$ **Midpoint** $= (-2, 1)$	10) $(2, 7), (10, -9)$ **Midpoint** $= (6, -1)$

Topic	**Finding Distance of Two Points**
Notes	✓ Use this formula to find the distance of two points A (x_1, y_1) and B (x_2, y_2): $$d = \sqrt{(x_2 - x_1)^2 + (y_2 - y_1)^2}$$
Example	*Find the distance of two points* $(-1, 5)$ and $(4, -7)$. Solution: *Use distance of two points formula:* $d = \sqrt{(x_2 - x_1)^2 + (y_2 - y_1)^2}$ $(x_1, y_1) = (-1, 5)$, and $(x_2, y_2) = (4, -7)$ Then: $d = \sqrt{(x_2 - x_1)^2 + (y_2 - y_1)^2} \rightarrow d = \sqrt{(4 - (-1))^2 + (-7 - 5)^2} = \sqrt{(5)^2 + (-12)^2} = \sqrt{25 + 144} = \sqrt{169} = 13$
Your Turn!	1) $(8, 2), (-6, 2)$ **Distance** = ____ 2) $(3, -4), (3, 6)$ **Distance** = ____ 3) $(-5, 10), (7, 1)$ **Distance** = ____ 4) $(8, 1), (-4, 6)$ **Distance** = ____ 5) $(-3, 6), (-4, 5)$ **Distance** = ____ 6) $(4, -1), (14, 23)$ **Distance** = ____ 7) $(3, 5), (6, 9)$ **Distance** = ____ 8) $(2, -2), (10, 4)$ **Distance** = ____

Find more at bit.ly/2KV50Hy

Topic	**Finding Distance of Two Points - Answers**
Notes	✓ Use this formula to find the distance of two points A (x_1, y_1) and B (x_2, y_2): $$d = \sqrt{(x_2 - x_1)^2 + (y_2 - y_1)^2}$$
Example	***Find the distance of two points*** $(-1, 5)$ and $(4, -7)$. **Solution: *Use distance of two points formula:*** $d = \sqrt{(x_2 - x_1)^2 + (y_2 - y_1)^2}$ $(x_1, y_1) = (-1, 5)$, and $(x_2, y_2) = (4, -7)$ Then: $d = \sqrt{(x_2 - x_1)^2 + (y_2 - y_1)^2} \rightarrow d = \sqrt{(4 - (-1))^2 + (-7 - 5)^2} = \sqrt{(5)^2 + (-12)^2} = \sqrt{25 + 144} = \sqrt{169} = 13$

Your Turn!	1) $(8, 2), (-6, 2)$ **Distance** $= 14$	2) $(3, -4), (3, 6)$ **Distance** $= 10$
	3) $(-5, 10), (7, 1)$ **Distance** $= 15$	4) $(8, 1), (-4, 6)$ **Distance** $= 13$
Find more at	5) $(-3, 6), (-4, 5)$ **Distance** $= \sqrt{2}$	6) $(4, -1), (14, 23)$ **Distance** $= 26$
bit.ly/2KV50Hy	7) $(3, 5), (6, 9)$ **Distance** $= 5$	8) $(2, -2), (10, 4)$ **Distance** $= 10$

Topic	**Multiplication Property of Exponents**
Notes	✓ Exponents are shorthand for repeated multiplication of the same number by itself. For example, instead of 2×2, we can write 2^2. For $3 \times 3 \times 3 \times 3$, we can write 3^4 ✓ In algebra, a variable is a letter used to stand for a number. The most common letters are: $x, y, z, a, b, c, m,$ and n. ✓ Exponent's rules: $x^a \times x^b = x^{a+b}$, $\frac{x^a}{x^b} = x^{a-b}$ $(x^a)^b = x^{a \times b}$ $(xy)^a = x^a \times y^a$ $(\frac{a}{b})^c = \frac{a^c}{b^c}$
Example	**Multiply.** $4x^3 \times 2x^2$ Use Exponent's rules: $x^a \times x^b = x^{a+b} \rightarrow x^3 \times x^2 = x^{3+2} = x^5$ Then: $4x^3 \times 2x^2 = 8x^5$

Your Turn!	1) $x^2 \times 5x =$	2) $3x^4 \times x^2 =$
	3) $3x^2 \times 4x^5 =$	4) $3x^2 \times 6xy =$
	5) $3x^5y \times 5x^2y^3 =$	6) $3x^2y^2 \times 5x^2y^8 =$
Find more at bit.ly/34AWHr1	7) $5x^2y \times 5x^2y^7 =$	8) $6x^6 \times 4x^9y^4 =$
	9) $4x^2y^5 \times 6x^5y^3 =$	10) $10x^6x^2 \times 7xy^5 =$

Topic	Multiplication Property of Exponents - Answers
Notes	✓ Exponents are shorthand for repeated multiplication of the same number by itself. For example, instead of 2×2, we can write 2^2. For $3 \times 3 \times 3 \times 3$, we can write 3^4 ✓ In algebra, a variable is a letter used to stand for a number. The most common letters are: $x, y, z, a, b, c, m, and\ n$. ✓ Exponent's rules: $x^a \times x^b = x^{a+b}$, $\frac{x^a}{x^b} = x^{a-b}$ $(x^a)^b = x^{a \times b}$ $(xy)^a = x^a \times y^a$ $(\frac{a}{b})^c = \frac{a^c}{b^c}$
Example	***Multiply.*** $4x^3 \times 2x^2$ Use Exponent's rules: $x^a \times x^b = x^{a+b} \rightarrow x^3 \times x^2 = x^{3+2} = x^5$ Then: $4x^3 \times 2x^2 = 8x^5$

Your Turn!		
	1) $x^2 \times 5x = 5x^3$	2) $3x^4 \times x^2 = 3x^6$
	3) $3x^2 \times 4x^5 = 12x^7$	4) $3x^2 \times 6xy = 18x^3y$
	5) $3x^5y \times 5x^2y^3 = 15x^7y^4$	6) $3x^2y^2 \times 5x^2y^8 = 15x^4y^{10}$
Find more at bit.ly/34AWHr1	7) $5x^2y \times 5x^2y^7 = 25x^4y^8$	8) $6x^6 \times 4x^9y^4 = 24x^{15}y^4$
	9) $4x^2y^5 \times 6x^5y^3 = 24x^7y^8$	10) $10x^6x^2 \times 7xy^5 = 70x^9y^5$

Topic	**Division Property of Exponents**
Notes	✓ For division of exponents use these formulas: $\frac{x^a}{x^b} = x^{a-b}$, $x \neq 0$ $\frac{x^a}{x^b} = \frac{1}{x^{b-a}}$, $x \neq 0$, $\qquad \frac{1}{x^b} = x^{-b}$
Example	*Simplify.* $\frac{6x^3y}{36x^2y^3}$ First cancel the common factor: $6 \rightarrow \frac{6x^3y}{36x^2y^3} = \frac{x^3y}{6x^2y^3}$ Use Exponent's rules: $\frac{x^a}{x^b} = x^{a-b} \rightarrow \frac{x^3}{x^2} = x^{3-2} = x^1 = x$ Then: $\frac{6x^3y}{36x^2y^3} = \frac{xy}{6y^3} \rightarrow$ now cancel the common factor: $y \rightarrow \frac{xy}{6y^3} = \frac{x}{6y^2}$

Your Turn!

1) $\frac{2^5}{2^2} =$ 　　　　2) $\frac{6x}{12x^3} =$

3) $\frac{3x^3}{2x^5} =$ 　　　　4) $\frac{12x^3}{14x^6} =$

5) $\frac{12x^3}{9y^8} =$ 　　　　6) $\frac{25xy^4}{5x^6y^2} =$

7) $\frac{2x^4y^5}{7xy^2} =$ 　　　　8) $\frac{16x^2y^8}{4x^3} =$

9) $\frac{9x^4}{12x^7y^9} =$ 　　　　10) $\frac{14y^8x^4}{21y^2x^8} =$

Find more at
bit.ly/37JAclZ

Topic	**Division Property of Exponents - Answers**
Notes	✓ For division of exponents use following formulas: $\frac{x^a}{x^b} = x^{a-b}$, $x \neq 0$ $\frac{x^a}{x^b} = \frac{1}{x^{b-a}}$, $x \neq 0$, $\qquad \frac{1}{x^b} = x^{-b}$
Example	**Simplify.** $\frac{6x^3y}{36x^2y^3}$ First cancel the common factor: $6 \rightarrow \frac{6x^3y}{36x^2y^3} = \frac{x^3y}{6x^2y^3}$ Use Exponent's rules: $\frac{x^a}{x^b} = x^{a-b} \rightarrow \frac{x^3}{x^2} = x^{3-2} = x^1 = x$ Then: $\frac{6x^3y}{36x^2y^3} = \frac{xy}{6y^3} \rightarrow$ now cancel the common factor: $y \rightarrow \frac{xy}{6y^3} = \frac{x}{6y^2}$

Your Turn!	1) $\frac{2^5}{2^2} = 2^3$	2) $\frac{6x}{12x^3} = \frac{1}{2x^2}$
	3) $\frac{3x^3}{2x^5} = \frac{3}{2x^2}$	4) $\frac{12x^3}{14x^6} = \frac{6}{7x^3}$
	5) $\frac{12x^3}{9y^8} = \frac{4x^3}{3y^8}$	6) $\frac{25xy^4}{5x^6y^2} = \frac{5y^2}{x^5}$
	7) $\frac{2x^4y^5}{7xy^2} = \frac{2x^3y^3}{7}$	8) $\frac{16x^2y^8}{4x^3} = \frac{4y^8}{x}$
Find more at bit.ly/37JAclZ	9) $\frac{9x^4}{12x^7y^9} = \frac{3}{4x^3y^9}$	10) $\frac{14y^8x^4}{21y^2x^8} = \frac{2y^6}{3x^4}$

Topic	Powers of Products and Quotients
Notes	✓ For any nonzero numbers a and b and any integer x, $$(ab)^x = a^x \times b^x, \left(\frac{a}{b}\right)^c = \frac{a^c}{b^c}$$
Example	**Simplify.** $\left(\frac{2x^3}{x}\right)^2$ First cancel the common factor: $x \rightarrow \left(\frac{2x^3}{x}\right)^2 = (2x^2)^2$ Use Exponent's rules: $(ab)^x = a^x \times b^x$ Then: $(2x^2)^2 = (2)^2(x^2)^2 = 4x^4$

Your Turn!		
	1) $(3x^3 x^3)^3 =$	2) $(2x^3 \times 6x)^2 =$
	3) $(10x^{11}y^3)^2 =$	4) $(9x^7 y^5)^2 =$
	5) $(4x^4 y^6)^3 =$	6) $(3x \times 4y^3)^2 =$
	7) $\left(\frac{5x}{x^2}\right)^2 =$	8) $\left(\frac{x^4 y^4}{x^2 y^2}\right)^3 =$
	9) $\left(\frac{24x}{4x^6}\right)^2 =$	10) $\left(\frac{x^6}{x^4 y^2}\right)^2 =$

Find more at

bit.ly/34CgPJm

Topic	Powers of Products and Quotients - Answers
Notes	✓ For any nonzero numbers a and b and any integer x, $$(ab)^x = a^x \times b^x, \left(\frac{a}{b}\right)^c = \frac{a^c}{b^c}$$
Example	*Simplify.* $\left(\frac{2x^3}{x}\right)^2$ First cancel the common factor: $x \rightarrow \left(\frac{2x^3}{x}\right)^2 = (2x^2)^2$ Use Exponent's rules: $(ab)^x = a^x \times b^x$ Then: $(2x^2)^2 = (2)^2(x^2)^2 = 4x^4$

Your Turn!		
	1) $(3x^3x^3)^3 = 27x^{18}$	2) $(2x^3 \times 6x)^2 = 144x^8$
	3) $(10x^{11}y^3)^2 =$ $100x^{22}y^6$	4) $(9x^7y^5)^2 = 81x^{14}y^{10}$
	5) $(4x^4y^6)^3 = 64\,x^{12}y^{18}$	6) $(3x \times 4y^3)^2 = 144x^2y^6$
Find more at bit.ly/34CgPJm	7) $\left(\frac{5x}{x^2}\right)^2 = \frac{25}{x^2}$	8) $\left(\frac{x^4y^4}{x^2y^2}\right)^3 = x^6y^6$
	9) $\left(\frac{24x}{4x^6}\right)^2 = \frac{36}{x^{10}}$	10) $\left(\frac{x^6}{x^4y^2}\right)^2 = \frac{x^4}{y^4}$

Topic	**Zero and Negative Exponents**
Notes	✓ A negative exponent is the reciprocal of that number with a positive exponent. $(3)^{-2} = \frac{1}{3^2}$ ✓ Zero-Exponent Rule: $a^0 = 1$, this means that anything raised to the zero power is 1. For example: $(28x^2y)^0 = 1$
Example	***Evaluate.*** $\left(\frac{1}{3}\right)^{-2} =$ Use negative exponent's rule: $\left(\frac{1}{x^a}\right)^{-2} = (x^a)^2 \rightarrow \left(\frac{1}{3}\right)^{-2} = (3)^2 =$ Then: $(3)^2 = 9$

Your Turn!	1) $2^{-4} =$	2) $4^{-3} =$
	3) $7^{-3} =$	4) $1^{-3} =$
	5) $8^{-3} =$	6) $4^{-4} =$
Find more at bit.ly/3rnkh4	7) $10^{-3} =$	8) $7^{-4} =$
	9) $\left(\frac{1}{6}\right)^{-1} =$	10) $\left(\frac{1}{9}\right)^{-2} =$

Topic	Zero and Negative Exponents - Answers
Notes	✓ A negative exponent is the reciprocal of that number with a positive exponent. $(3)^{-2} = \frac{1}{3^2}$ ✓ Zero-Exponent Rule: $a^0 = 1$, this means that anything raised to the zero power is 1. For example: $(28x^2y)^0 = 1$
Example	*Evaluate.* $\left(\frac{1}{3}\right)^{-2} =$ Use negative exponent's rule: $\left(\frac{1}{x^a}\right)^{-2} = (x^a)^2 \rightarrow \left(\frac{1}{3}\right)^{-2} = (3)^2 =$ Then: $(3)^2 = 9$

Your Turn!		
	1) $2^{-4} = \frac{1}{16}$	2) $4^{-3} = \frac{1}{64}$
	3) $7^{-3} = \frac{1}{343}$	4) $1^{-3} = 1$
	5) $8^{-3} = \frac{1}{512}$	6) $4^{-4} = \frac{1}{256}$
	7) $10^{-3} = \frac{1}{1,000}$	8) $7^{-4} = \frac{1}{2,401}$
	9) $\left(\frac{1}{6}\right)^{-1} = 6$	10) $\left(\frac{1}{9}\right)^{-2} = 81$

Find more at

bit.ly/3rnkh4

Topic	**Negative Exponents and Negative Bases**
Notes	✓ Make the power positive. A negative exponent is the reciprocal of that number with a positive exponent. ✓ The parenthesis is important! 5^{-2} is not the same as $(-5)^{-2}$ $$(-5)^{-2} = -\frac{1}{5^2} \text{ and } (-5)^{-2} = +\frac{1}{5^2}$$
Example	*Simplify.* $\left(-\frac{3x}{4yz}\right)^{-3} =$ Use negative exponent's rule: $\left(\frac{x^a}{x^b}\right)^{-2} = \left(\frac{x^b}{x^a}\right)^2 \rightarrow \left(-\frac{3x}{4yz}\right)^{-3} = \left(-\frac{4yz}{3x}\right)^3$ Now use exponent's rule: $\left(\frac{a}{b}\right)^c = \frac{a^c}{b^c} \rightarrow \left(-\frac{4yz}{3x}\right)^3 = -\frac{4^3 y^3 z^3}{3^3 x^3} = -\frac{64 y^3 z^3}{27 x^3}$
Your Turn! **Find more at** bit.ly/3nPROSM	1) $-4x^{-3}y^{-3} =$ 2) $25x^{-4}y^{-2} =$ 3) $14a^{-6}b^{-7} =$ 4) $-12x^2 y^{-3} =$ 5) $-\dfrac{25}{x^{-6}} =$ 6) $\dfrac{7b}{-9c^{-4}} =$ 7) $\dfrac{7ab}{a^{-3}b^{-1}} =$ 8) $-\dfrac{5n^{-2}}{10p^{-3}} = -$ 9) $\dfrac{36ab^{-1}}{-3c^{-2}} =$ 10) $\left(\dfrac{5a}{3c}\right)^{-2} =$

Topic	Negative Exponents and Negative Bases - Answers
Notes	✓ Make the power positive. A negative exponent is the reciprocal of that number with a positive exponent. ✓ The parenthesis is important! 5^{-2} is not the same as $(-\ 5)^{-2}$ $$(-\ 5)^{-2} = -\frac{1}{5^2} \text{ and } (-5)^{-2} = +\frac{1}{5^2}$$
Example	*Simplify.* $\left(-\frac{3x}{4yz}\right)^{-3} =$ Use negative exponent's rule: $\left(\frac{x^a}{x^b}\right)^{-2} = \left(\frac{x^b}{x^a}\right)^2 \rightarrow \left(-\frac{3x}{4yz}\right)^{-3} = \left(-\frac{4yz}{3x}\right)^3$ Now use exponent's rule: $\left(\frac{a}{b}\right)^c = \frac{a^c}{b^c} \rightarrow \left(-\frac{4yz}{3x}\right)^3 = -\frac{4^3y^3z^3}{3^3x^3} = -\frac{64y^3z^3}{27x^3}$

Your Turn!		
	1) $-4x^{-3}y^{-3} = -\frac{4}{x^3\,y^3}$	2) $25x^{-4}y^{-2} = \frac{25}{x^4y^2}$
	3) $14a^{-6}b^{-7} = \frac{14}{a^6b^7}$	4) $-12x^2y^{-3} = -\frac{12x^2}{y^3}$
	5) $-\frac{25}{x^{-6}} = -25x^6$	6) $\frac{7b}{-9c^{-4}} = -\frac{7bc^4}{9}$
Find more at bit.ly/3nPROSM	7) $\frac{7ab}{a^{-3}b^{-1}} = 7a^4b^2$	8) $-\frac{5n^{-2}}{10p^{-3}} = -\frac{p^3}{2n^2}$
	9) $\frac{36ab^{-1}}{-3c^{-2}} = -\frac{12ac^2}{b}$	10) $\left(\frac{5a}{3c}\right)^{-2} = \frac{9c^2}{25a^2}$

Topic	Scientific Notation
Notes	✓ It is used to write very big or very small numbers in decimal form. ✓ In scientific notation all numbers are written in the form of: $$m \times 10^n$$ **Decimal notation** **Scientific notation** 3 $\qquad\qquad$ 3×10^0 $-45,000$ $\qquad$ -4.5×10^4 0.3 $\qquad\qquad$ 3×10^{-1} 2,122.456 $\qquad$ 2.122456×10^3
Example	**Write 0.00054 in scientific notation.** First, move the decimal point to the right so that you have a number that is between 1 and 10. Then: $m = 5.4$ Now, determine how many places the decimal moved in step 1 by the power of 10. Then: $10^{-4} \rightarrow$ When the decimal moved to the right, the exponent is negative. Then: $0.00054 = 5.4 \times 10^{-4}$

Your Turn!		
	1) $0.000452 =$	2) $0.00016 =$
	3) $52,000,000 =$	4) $21,000 =$
Find more at bit.ly/3nOwJYP	5) $3 \times 10^{-1} =$	6) $5 \times 10^{-2} =$
	7) $1.4 \times 10^4 =$	8) $3 \times 10^{-5} =$

Topic	Scientific Notation – Answers
Notes	✓ It is used to write very big or very small numbers in decimal form. ✓ In scientific notation all numbers are written in the form of: $$m \times 10^n$$ <table><tr><td>**Decimal notation**</td><td>**Scientific notation**</td></tr><tr><td>3</td><td>3×10^0</td></tr><tr><td>$-45,000$</td><td>-4.5×10^4</td></tr><tr><td>0.3</td><td>3×10^{-1}</td></tr><tr><td>2,122.456</td><td>2.122456×10^3</td></tr></table>
Example	*Write 0.00054 in scientific notation.* First, move the decimal point to the right so that you have a number that is between 1 and 10. Then: $m = 5.4$ Now, determine how many places the decimal moved in step 1 by the power of 10. Then: $10^{-4} \rightarrow$ When the decimal moved to the right, the exponent is negative. Then: $0.00054 = 5.4 \times 10^{-4}$

Your Turn!		
	1) $0.000452 = 4.52 \times 10^{-4}$	2) $0.00016 = 1.6 \times 10^{-4}$
	3) $52,000,000 = 5.2 \times 10^7$	4) $21,000 = 2.1 \times 10^4$
Find more at bit.ly/3nOwJYP	5) $3 \times 10^{-1} = 0.3$	6) $5 \times 10^{-2} = 0.05$
	7) $1.4 \times 10^4 = 14,000$	8) $3 \times 10^{-5} = 0.00003$

Topic	Radicals
Notes	✓ If n is a positive integer and x is a real number, then: $\sqrt[n]{x} = x^{\frac{1}{n}}$, $\sqrt[n]{xy} = x^{\frac{1}{n}} \times y^{\frac{1}{n}}$, $\sqrt[n]{\frac{x}{y}} = \frac{x^{\frac{1}{n}}}{y^{\frac{1}{n}}}$, and $\sqrt[n]{x} \times \sqrt[n]{y} = \sqrt[n]{xy}$ ✓ A square root of x is a number r whose square is: $r^2 = x$ (r is a square root of x. ✓ To add and subtract radicals, we need to have the same values under the radical. For example: $\sqrt{3} + \sqrt{3} = 2\sqrt{3}$, $3\sqrt{5} - \sqrt{5} = 2\sqrt{5}$
Example	*Evaluate*. $\sqrt{32} + \sqrt{8} =$ **Solution:** Since we do not have the same values under the radical, we cannot add these two radicals. But we can simplify each radical. $\sqrt{32} = \sqrt{16} \times \sqrt{2} = 4\sqrt{2}$ and $\sqrt{8} = \sqrt{4} \times \sqrt{2} = 2\sqrt{2}$ Now, we have the same values under the radical. Then: $$\sqrt{32} + \sqrt{8} = 4\sqrt{2} + 2\sqrt{2} = 6\sqrt{2}$$

Your Turn!		
Find more at bit.ly/2WEATqr	1) $\sqrt{6} \times \sqrt{6} =$	2) $\sqrt{12} \times \sqrt{3} =$
	3) $\sqrt{3} \times \sqrt{27} =$	4) $\sqrt{32} \div \sqrt{2} =$
	5) $\sqrt{2} + \sqrt{8} =$	6) $\sqrt{27} - \sqrt{3} =$
	7) $3\sqrt{7} - 2\sqrt{7} =$	8) $6\sqrt{5} \times 3\sqrt{5} =$

Topic	Radicals - Answers
Notes	✓ If n is a positive integer and x is a real number, then: $\sqrt[n]{x} = x^{\frac{1}{n}}$, $\sqrt[n]{xy} = x^{\frac{1}{n}} \times y^{\frac{1}{n}}$, $\sqrt[n]{\frac{x}{y}} = \frac{x^{\frac{1}{n}}}{y^{\frac{1}{n}}}$, and $\sqrt[n]{x} \times \sqrt[n]{y} = \sqrt[n]{xy}$ ✓ A square root of x is a number r whose square is: $r^2 = x$ (r is a square root of x. ✓ To add and subtract radicals, we need to have the same values under the radical. For example: $\sqrt{3} + \sqrt{3} = 2\sqrt{3}$, $3\sqrt{5} - \sqrt{5} = 2\sqrt{5}$
Example	*Evaluate.* $\sqrt{32} + \sqrt{8} =$ **Solution:** Since we do not have the same values under the radical, we cannot add these two radicals. But we can simplify each radical. $\sqrt{32} = \sqrt{16} \times \sqrt{2} = 4\sqrt{2}$ and $\sqrt{8} = \sqrt{4} \times \sqrt{2} = 2\sqrt{2}$ Now, we have the same values under the radical. Then: $$\sqrt{32} + \sqrt{8} = 4\sqrt{2} + 2\sqrt{2} = 6\sqrt{2}$$

Your Turn!		
Find more at bit.ly/2WEATqr	1) $\sqrt{6} \times \sqrt{6} = 6$	2) $\sqrt{12} \times \sqrt{3} = 6$
	3) $\sqrt{3} \times \sqrt{27} = 9$	4) $\sqrt{32} \div \sqrt{2} = 4$
	5) $\sqrt{2} + \sqrt{8} = 3\sqrt{2}$	6) $\sqrt{27} - \sqrt{3} = 2\sqrt{3}$
	7) $3\sqrt{7} - 2\sqrt{7} = \sqrt{7}$	8) $6\sqrt{5} \times 3\sqrt{5} = 90$

Topic	**Simplifying Polynomials**
Notes	✓ Find "like" terms. (they have same variables with same power). ✓ Use "FOIL". (First–Out–In–Last) for binomials: $$(x + a)(x + b) = x^2 + (b + a)x + ab$$ ✓ Add or Subtract "like" terms using order of operation.
Example	**Simplify this expression.** $(x + 3)(x - 8) =$ **Solution:** First apply FOIL method: $(a + b)(c + d) = ac + ad + bc + bd$ $(x + 3)(x - 8) = x^2 - 8x + 3x - 24$ Now combine like terms: $x^2 - 8x + 3x - 24 = x^2 - 5x - 24$

Your Turn!

1) $-(4x - 3) =$

_____

2) $3(4x + 7) =$

_____

3) $3x(3x - 4) =$

_____

4) $5x(2x + 8) =$

_____

5) $-2x(5x + 6) + 5x =$

_____

6) $-4x(8x - 3) - x^2 =$

_____

7) $(x + 4)(x + 5) =$

_____

8) $(x + 2)(x + 8) =$

_____

9) $-5x^2 + 9x^3 + 10x^2 =$

_____

10) $-6x^5 + 8x^4 + 9x^5 =$

_____

Find more at

bit.ly/3rnAcj8

Topic	Simplifying Polynomials – Answers
Notes	✓ Find "like" terms. (they have same variables with same power). ✓ Use "FOIL". (First–Out–In–Last) for binomials: $$(x + a)(x + b) = x^2 + (b + a)x + ab$$ ✓ Add or Subtract "like" terms using order of operation.
Example	*Simplify this expression*. $(x + 3)(x - 8) =$ **Solution:** First apply FOIL method: $(a + b)(c + d) = ac + ad + bc + bd$ $(x + 3)(x - 8) = x^2 - 8x + 3x - 24$ Now combine like terms: $x^2 - 8x + 3x - 24 = x^2 - 5x - 24$

Your Turn!		
	1) $-(4x - 3) =$ $-4x + 3$	2) $3(4x + 7) =$ $12x + 21$
	3) $3x(3x - 4) =$ $9x^2 - 12x$	4) $5x(2x + 8) =$ $10x^2 + 40x$
	5) $-2x(5x + 6) + 5x =$ $-10x^2 - 7x$	6) $-4x(8x - 3) - x^2 =$ $-33x^2 + 12x$
	7) $(x + 4)(x + 5) =$ $x^2 + 9x + 20$	8) $(x + 2)(x + 8) =$ $x^2 + 10x + 16$
	9) $-5x^2 + 9x^3 + 10x^2 =$ $9x^3 + 5x^2$	10) $-6x^5 + 8x^4 + 9x^5 =$ $3x^5 + 8x^4$

Find more at

bit.ly/3rnAcj8

Topic	**Adding and Subtracting Polynomials**
Notes	✓ Adding polynomials is just a matter of combining like terms, with some order of operations considerations thrown in. ✓ Be careful with the minus signs, and don't confuse addition and multiplication!
Example	***Simplify the expressions.*** $(3x^2 - 4x^3) - (5x^3 - 8x^2) =$ **Solution:** First use Distributive Property: $-(5x^3 - 8x^2) = -5x^3 + 8x^2$ $\rightarrow (3x^2 - 4x^3) - (5x^3 - 8x^2) = 3x^2 - 4x^3 - 5x^3 + 8x^2$ Now combine like terms: $3x^2 - 4x^3 - 5x^3 + 8x^2 = -9x^3 + 11x^2$

Your Turn!

1) $(x^2 - 3x) + (2x^2 - 6) =$
_____

2) $(4x^3 + 2x) - (x^3 + 5) =$
_____

3) $(x^2 - 5x) + (6x^2 - 5) =$
_____

4) $(8x^2 - 2) - (3x^2 + 7) =$
_____

5) $(3x^2 + 2) - (2 - 4x^2) =$
_____

6) $(x^3 + x^2) - (x^3 - 10) =$
_____

7) $(3x^3 - 2x) - (x - x^3) =$
_____

8) $(x - 5x^4) - (2x^4 + 3x) =$
_____

Find more at

bit.ly/2KUqHqQ

9) $(8x^3 + 3) - (5 - 4x^3) =$
_____

10) $(9x^2 + 4x^3) - (3x^3 + 2) =$
_____

Topic	Adding and Subtracting Polynomials – Answers
Notes	✓ Adding polynomials is just a matter of combining like terms, with some order of operations considerations thrown in. ✓ Be careful with the minus signs, and don't confuse addition and multiplication!
Example	***Simplify the expressions.*** $(3x^2 - 4x^3) - (5x^3 - 8x^2) =$ **Solution:** First use Distributive Property: $-(5x^3 - 8x^2) = -5x^3 + 8x^2$ $\rightarrow (3x^2 - 4x^3) - (5x^3 - 8x^2) = 3x^2 - 4x^3 - 5x^3 + 8x^2$ Now combine like terms: $3x^2 - 4x^3 - 5x^3 + 8x^2 = -9x^3 + 11x^2$

Your Turn!		
Find more at bit.ly/2KUqHqQ	1) $(x^2 - 3x) + (2x^2 - 6) =$ $3x^2 - 3x - 6$	2) $(4x^3 + 2x) - (x^3 + 5) =$ $3x^3 + 2x - 5$
	3) $(x^2 - 5x) + (6x^2 - 5) =$ $7x^2 - 5x - 5$	4) $(8x^2 - 2) - (3x^2 + 7) =$ $5x^2 - 9$
	5) $(3x^2 + 2) - (2 - 4x^2) =$ $7x^2$	6) $(x^3 + x^2) - (x^3 - 10) =$ $x^2 + 10$
	7) $(3x^3 - 2x) - (x - x^3) =$ $4x^3 - 3x$	8) $(x - 5x^4) - (2x^4 + 3x) =$ $-7x^4 - 2x$
	9) $(8x^3 + 3) - (5 - 4x^3) =$ $12x^3 - 2$	10) $(9x^2 + 4x^3) - (3x^3 + 2) =$ $x^3 + 9x^2 - 2$

Topic	**Multiplying Binomials**
Notes	✓A binomial is a polynomial that is the sum or the difference of two terms, each of which is a monomial. ✓To multiply two binomials, use "FOIL" method. (First–Out–In–Last) $(x + a)(x + b) = x \times x + x \times b + a \times x + a \times b = x^2 + bx + ax + ab$
Example	*Multiply.* $(x - 4)(x + 9) =$ **Solution:** Use "FOIL". (First–Out–In–Last): $(x - 4)(x + 9) = x^2 + 9x - 4x - 36$ Then simplify: $x^2 + 9x - 4x - 36 = x^2 + 5x - 36$
Your Turn!	1) $(x + 4)(x + 4) =$ _____ 2) $(x + 4)(x + 3) =$ _____ 3) $(x - 3)(x + 4) =$ _____ 4) $(x - 2)(x - 4) =$ _____ 5) $(x + 3)(x + 4) =$ _____ 6) $(x + 5)(x + 4) =$ _____ 7) $(x - 6)(x - 5) =$ _____ 8) $(x - 5)(x - 5) =$ _____ 9) $(x + 3)(x - 5) =$ _____ 10) $(x - 6)(x + 4) =$ _____

Find more at

bit.lv/3aCsOFL

Topic	Multiplying Binomials – Answers
Notes	✓ A binomial is a polynomial that is the sum or the difference of two terms, each of which is a monomial. ✓ To multiply two binomials, use "FOIL" method. (First–Out–In–Last) $(x + a)(x + b) = x \times x + x \times b + a \times x + a \times b = x^2 + bx + ax + ab$
Example	*Multiply.* $(x - 4)(x + 9) =$ **Solution:** Use "FOIL". (First–Out–In–Last): $(x - 4)(x + 9) = x^2 + 9x - 4x - 36$ Then simplify: $x^2 + 9x - 4x - 36 = x^2 + 5x - 36$

Your Turn!	1) $(x + 4)(x + 4) =$ $x^2 + 8x + 16$	2) $(x + 4)(x + 3) =$ $x^2 + 7x + 12$
	3) $(x - 3)(x + 4) =$ $x^2 + x - 12$	4) $(x - 2)(x - 4) =$ $x^2 - 6x + 8$
	5) $(x + 3)(x + 4) =$ $x^2 + 7x + 12$	6) $(x + 5)(x + 4) =$ $x^2 + 9x + 20$
Find more at bit.ly/3aCsOFL	7) $(x - 6)(x - 5) =$ $x^2 - 11x + 30$	8) $(x - 5)(x - 5) =$ $x^2 - 10x + 25$
	9) $(x + 3)(x - 5) =$ $x^2 - 2x - 15$	10) $(x - 6)(x + 4) =$ $x^2 - 2x - 24$

Topic	**Multiplying and Dividing Monomials**
Notes	✓ When you divide or multiply two monomials you need to divide or multiply their coefficients and then divide or multiply their variables. ✓ In case of exponents with the same base, you need to subtract their powers. ✓ Exponent's rules: $$x^a \times x^b = x^{a+b}, \qquad \frac{x^a}{x^b} = x^{a-b}$$ $$\frac{1}{x^b} = x^{-b}, \quad (x^a)^b = x^{a \times b}$$ $$(xy)^a = x^a \times y^a$$
Example	***Divide expressions.*** $\frac{-18x^5y^6}{2xy^2} =$ **Solution:** Use exponents' division rule: $\frac{x^a}{x^b} = x^{a-b}$, $\frac{x^5}{x} = x^{5-1} = x^4$ and $\frac{y^6}{y^2} = y^4$ Then: $\frac{-18x^5y^6}{2xy^2} = -9x^4y^4$
Your Turn!	1) $(x^6y)(xy^3) =$ _____ 2) $(x^5y^2)(x^3y^3) =$ _____ 3) $(x^7y^4)(2x^5y^2) =$ _____ 4) $(3x^5y^4)(4x^6y^3) =$ _____ 5) $(-6x^8y^7)(4x^6y^9) =$ _____ 6) $(-2x^9y^3)(9x^7y^8) =$ _____ **Find more at** bit.ly/2WHp4Q4 7) $\frac{40x^9y^6}{8x^5y^4} =$ _____ 8) $\frac{-56x^{10}y^{15}}{8x^8y^9} =$ _____

Topic	Multiplying and Dividing Monomials - Answers
Notes	✓ When you divide or multiply two monomials you need to divide or multiply their coefficients and then divide or multiply their variables. ✓ In case of exponents with the same base, you need to subtract their powers. ✓ Exponent's rules: $$x^a \times x^b = x^{a+b}, \qquad \frac{x^a}{x^b} = x^{a-b}$$ $$\frac{1}{x^b} = x^{-b}, \quad (x^a)^b = x^{a \times b}$$ $$(xy)^a = x^a \times y^a$$
Example	*Divide expressions.* $\frac{-18x^5y^6}{2xy^2} =$ **Solution:** Use exponents' division rule: $\frac{x^a}{x^b} = x^{a-b}, \frac{x^5}{x} = x^{5-1} = x^4$ and $\frac{y^6}{y^2} = y^4$ Then: $\frac{-18x^5y^6}{2xy^2} = -9x^4y^4$

Your Turn!	1) $(x^6y)(xy^3) =$ x^7y^4	2) $(x^5y^2)(x^3y^3) =$ x^8y^5
	3) $(x^7y^4)(2x^5y^2) =$ $2x^{12}y^6$	4) $(3x^5y^4)(4x^6y^3) =$ $12x^{11}y^7$
	5) $(-6x^8y^7)(4x^6y^9) =$ $-24x^{14}y^{16}$	6) $(-2x^9y^3)(9x^7y^8) =$ $-18x^{16}y^{11}$
Find more at bit.ly/2WHp4Q4	7) $\frac{40x^9y^6}{8x^5y^4} =$ $5x^4y^2$	8) $\frac{-56x^{10}y^{15}}{8x^8y^9} =$ $-7x^2y^6$

Topic	**Multiplying a Polynomial and a Monomial**
Notes	✓ When multiplying monomials, use the product rule for exponents. $x^a \times x^b = x^{a+b}$ ✓ When multiplying a monomial by a polynomial, use the distributive property. $$a \times (b + c) = a \times b + a \times c = ab + ac$$ $$a \times (b - c) = a \times b - a \times c = ab - ac$$
Example	***Multiply expressions.*** $4x(5x - 8) =$ **Solution:** Use Distributive Property: $4x(5x - 8) = 4x \times 5x - 4x \times (8) =$ Now, simplify: $4x \times 5x - 4x \times (8) = 20x^2 - 32x$

Your Turn!	1) $4x(3x + y) =$ _____	2) $x(x - 6y) =$ _____
	3) $-x(5x - 3y) =$ _____	4) $4x(x + 5y) =$ _____
	5) $-x(5x + 8y) =$ _____	6) $2x(6x - 7y) =$ _____
Find more at bit.ly/3aBYdx2	7) $-4x(x^3 + 3y^2 - 7x) =$ _____	8) $6x(x^2 - 4y^2 + 3) =$ _____

Topic	Multiplying a Polynomial and a Monomial - Answers
Notes	✓ When multiplying monomials, use the product rule for exponents. $x^a \times x^b = x^{a+b}$ ✓ When multiplying a monomial by a polynomial, use the distributive property. $$a \times (b + c) = a \times b + a \times c = ab + ac$$ $$a \times (b - c) = a \times b - a \times c = ab - ac$$
Example	***Multiply expressions.*** $4x(5x - 8) =$ **Solution:** Use Distributive Property: $4x(5x - 8) = 4x \times 5x - 4x \times (8) =$ Now, simplify: $4x \times 5x - 4x \times (8) = 20x^2 - 32x$

Your Turn!		
	1) $4x(3x + y) =$ $12x^2 + 4xy$	2) $x(x - 6y) =$ $x^2 - 6xy$
	3) $-x(5x - 3y) =$ $-5x^2 + 3xy$	4) $4x(x + 5y) =$ $4x^2 + 20xy$
	5) $-x(5x + 8y) =$ $-5x^2 - 8xy$	6) $2x(6x - 7y) =$ $12x^2 - 14xy$
	7) $-4x(x^3 + 3y^2 - 7x) =$ $-4x^4 - 12xy^2 + 28x^2$	8) $6x(x^2 - 4y^2 + 3) =$ $6x^3 - 24xy^2 + 18x$

Find more at

bit.ly/3aBYdx2

Topic	**Multiplying Monomials**
Notes	✓ A monomial is a polynomial with just one term: Examples: $5x$ or $7x^2yz^8$. ✓ When you multiply monomials, first multiply the coefficients (a number placed before and multiplying the variable) and then multiply the variables using multiplication property of exponents. $x^a \times x^b = x^{a+b}$
Example	***Multiply.*** $(-3xy^4z^5) \times (2x^2y^5z^2) =$ **Solution:** Multiply coefficients and find same variables and use multiplication property of exponents: $x^a \times x^b = x^{a+b}$ $-3 \times 2 = -6,\ x \times x^2 = x^{1+2} = x^3,\ y^4 \times y^5 = y^{4+5} = y^9$, and $z^2 \times z^5 = z^{2+5} = z^7$ Then: $(-3xy^4z^5) \times (2x^2y^5z^2) = -6x^3y^9z^7$

Your Turn!	1) $3x^2 \times 5x^6 =$ _____	2) $6x^7 \times 2x^4 =$ _____
	3) $-2x^2y^4 \times 6x^3y^2 =$ _____	4) $-5x^5y \times 3x^3y^4 =$ _____
	5) $8x^7y^5 \times 5x^6y^3 =$ _____	6) $-6x^7y^5 \times (-3x^9y^8) =$ _____
Find more at bit.ly/2KLVoP8	7) $14x^8y^8z^4 \times 2x^4y^3z =$ _____	8) $-7x^9y^7z^{11} \times 6x^6y^7z^5 =$ _____

Topic	Multiplying Monomials- Answers
Notes	✓ A monomial is a polynomial with just one term: Examples: $5x$ or $7x^2yz^8$. ✓ When you multiply monomials, first multiply the coefficients (a number placed before and multiplying the variable) and then multiply the variables using multiplication property of exponents. $x^a \times x^b = x^{a+b}$
Example	**Multiply.** $(-3xy^4z^5) \times (2x^2y^5z^2) =$ **Solution:** Multiply coefficients and find same variables and use multiplication property of exponents: $x^a \times x^b = x^{a+b}$ $-3 \times 2 = -6$, $x \times x^2 = x^{1+2} = x^3$, $y^4 \times y^5 = y^{4+5} = y^9$, and $z^2 \times z^5 = z^{2+5} = z^7$ Then: $(-3xy^4z^5) \times (2x^2y^5z^2) = -6x^3y^9z^7$

Your Turn!		
	1) $3x^2 \times 5x^6 =$ $15x^8$	2) $6x^7 \times 2x^4 =$ $12x^{11}$
	3) $-2x^2y^4 \times 6x^3y^2 =$ $-12x^5y^6$	4) $-5x^5y \times 3x^3y^4 =$ $-15x^8y^5$
	5) $8x^7y^5 \times 5x^6y^3 =$ $40x^{13}y^8$	6) $-6x^7y^5 \times (-3x^9y^8) =$ $18x^{16}y^{13}$
	7) $14x^8y^8z^4 \times 2x^4y^3z =$ $28x^{12}y^{11}z^5$	8) $-7x^9y^7z^{11} \times 6x^6y^7z^5 =$ $-42x^{15}y^{14}z^{16}$

Find more at

bit.ly/2KLVoP8

Topic	Factoring Trinomials
Notes	To factor trinomial, use of the following methods: ✓ "FOIL": $(x + a)(x + b) = x^2 + (b + a)x + ab$ ✓ "Difference of Squares": $$a^2 - b^2 = (a + b)(a - b)$$ $$a^2 + 2ab + b^2 = (a + b)(a + b)$$ $$a^2 - 2ab + b^2 = (a - b)(a - b)$$ ✓ "Reverse FOIL": $x^2 + (b + a)x + ab = (x + a)(x + b)$
Example	**Factor this trinomial.** $x^2 + 12x + 32 =$ **Solution:** Break the expression into groups: $(x^2 + 4x) + (8x + 32)$ Now factor out x from $x^2 + 4x$: $x(x + 4)$, and factor out 8 from $8x + 32$: $8(x + 4)$ Then: $(x^2 + 4x) + (8x + 32) = x(x + 4) + 8(x + 4)$ Now factor out like term: $(x + 4) \rightarrow (x + 4)(x + 8)$

Your Turn!

1) $x^2 + 3x - 4 =$ _____	2) $x^2 + 4x - 12 =$ _____
3) $x^2 + x - 12 =$ _____	4) $x^2 - 6x + 8 =$ _____
5) $x^2 + 7x + 12 =$ _____	6) $x^2 + 12x + 32 =$ _____
7) $x^2 + 13x + 30 =$ _____	8) $x^2 - x + 72 =$ _____

Find more at

bit.ly/38EpdJA

Topic	Factoring Trinomials – Answers
Notes	To factor trinomial, use of the following methods: ✓ "FOIL": $(x + a)(x + b) = x^2 + (b + a)x + ab$ ✓ "Difference of Squares": $$a^2 - b^2 = (a + b)(a - b)$$ $$a^2 + 2ab + b^2 = (a + b)(a + b)$$ $$a^2 - 2ab + b^2 = (a - b)(a - b)$$ ✓ "Reverse FOIL": $x^2 + (b + a)x + ab = (x + a)(x + b)$
Example	***Factor this trinomial.*** $x^2 + 12x + 32 =$ **Solution:** Break the expression into groups: $(x^2 + 4x) + (8x + 32)$ Now factor out x from $x^2 + 4x$: $x(x + 4)$, and factor out 8 from $8x + 32$: $8(x + 4)$ Then: $(x^2 + 4x) + (8x + 32) = x(x + 4) + 8(x + 4)$ Now factor out like term: $(x + 4) \rightarrow (x + 4)(x + 8)$

Your Turn!	1) $x^2 + 3x - 4 =$ $(x + 4)(x - 1)$	2) $x^2 + 4x - 12 =$ $(x - 2)(x + 6)$
	3) $x^2 + x - 12 =$ $(x - 3)(x + 4)$	4) $x^2 - 6x + 8 =$ $(x - 2)(x - 4)$
Find more at bit.ly/38EpdJA	5) $x^2 + 7x + 12 =$ $(x + 3)(x + 4)$	6) $x^2 + 12x + 32 =$ $(x + 8)(x + 4)$
	7) $x^2 + 13x + 30 =$ $(x + 10)(x + 3)$	8) $x^2 - x - 72 =$ $(x - 9)(x + 8)$

Topic	The Pythagorean Theorem
Notes	✓ In any right triangle: $a^2 + b^2 = c^2$
Example	Right triangle ABC (not shown) has two legs of lengths 18 cm (AB) and 24 cm (AC). What is the length of the third side (BC)? **Solution:** Use Pythagorean Theorem: $a^2 + b^2 = c^2$ Then: $a^2 + b^2 = c^2$ → $18^2 + 24^2 = c^2$ → $324 + 576 = c^2$ $c^2 = 900$ → $c = \sqrt{900} = 30\ cm$
Your Turn! **Find more at** bit.lv/37Jl08v 	1) _____ 2) _____ 3) _____ 4) _____

Topic	The Pythagorean Theorem – Answers
Notes	✓ In any right triangle: $a^2 + b^2 = c^2$
Example	Right triangle ABC (not shown) has two legs of lengths 18 cm (AB) and 24 cm (AC). What is the length of the third side (BC)? **Solution:** Use Pythagorean Theorem: $a^2 + b^2 = c^2$ Then: $a^2 + b^2 = c^2 \rightarrow 18^2 + 24^2 = c^2 \rightarrow 324 + 576 = c^2$ $c^2 = 900 \rightarrow c = \sqrt{900} = 30\ cm$

Your Turn!

1) 10

2) 30

3) 12

4) 6

Find more at

bit.ly/37Jl08v

Topic	**Triangles**
Notes	✓ In any triangle the sum of all angles is 180 degrees. ✓ 0Area of a triangle = $\frac{1}{2}$ $(base \times height)$ *(diagram of triangle with height h and base b)*
Example	**What is the area of the following triangle?** *(right triangle with legs 6 and 16)* **Solution:** Use the area formula: Area = $\frac{1}{2}$ $(base \times height)$ $base = 16$ and $height = 6$ Area = $\frac{1}{2}(16 \times 6) = \frac{96}{2} = 48$

Your Turn!

1) _____

(right triangle with sides 20 and 12)

2) _____

(right triangle with sides 18 and 28)

3) _____

(right triangle with sides 20 and 30)

4) _____

(right triangle with sides 34 and 40)

Topic	Triangles – Answers
Notes	✓ In any triangle the sum of all angles is 180 degrees. ✓ Area of a triangle = $\frac{1}{2}(base \times height)$
Example	**What is the area of the following triangle?** **Solution:** Use the area formula: Area $= \frac{1}{2}(base \times height)$ $base = 16$ and $height = 6$ Area $= \frac{1}{2}(16 \times 6) = \frac{96}{2} = 48$

Your Turn!	1) 120	2) 252
	20 12	18 28
Find more at bit.ly/3haZrRg	3) 300 20 30	4) 680 34 40

Topic	Polygons
Notes	Perimeter of a square $= 4 \times side = 4s$ Perimeter of a rectangle $= 2(width + length)$ Perimeter of trapezoid $= a + b + c + d$ Perimeter of a regular hexagon $= 6a$ Perimeter of a parallelogram $= 2(l + w)$
Example	*Find the perimeter of following regular hexagon.* **Solution:** Since the hexagon is regular, all sides are equal. Then: Perimeter of Hexagon $= 6 \times (one\ side)$ Perimeter of Hexagon $= 6 \times (one\ side) = 6 \times 9 = 54\ m$

Your Turn!

5) *(rectangle)* _____

8 *in*

12 *in*

6) _____

8 *m*

10 *m*   10 *m*

14 *m*

Find more at

bit.ly/3nFNiGi

7) *(regular hexagon)*_____
5 *m*

8) *(parallelogram)*_____

9 *in*

11 *in*

Topic	Polygons – Answers
Notes	Perimeter of a square $= 4 \times side = 4s$ Perimeter of a rectangle $= 2(width + length)$ Perimeter of trapezoid $= a + b + c + d$ Perimeter of a regular hexagon $= 6a$ Perimeter of a parallelogram $= 2(l + w)$
Example	**Find the perimeter of following regular hexagon.** **Solution:** Since the hexagon is regular, all sides are equal. Then: Perimeter of Hexagon $= 6 \times (one\ side)$ Perimeter of Hexagon $= 6 \times (one\ side) = 6 \times 9 = 54\ m$
Your Turn!	5) *(rectangle)* 40 *in* 8 *in* 12 *in* 6) 42 *m* 8 *m* 10 *m* 10 *m* 14 *m*
Find more at bit.ly/3nFNiGi	7) *(regular hexagon)* 30 *m* 5 *m* 8) *(parallelogram)* 40 *in* 9 *in* 11 *in*

Topic	Circles
Notes	✓ In a circle, variable r is usually used for the radius and d for diameter and π is about 3.14. ✓ *Area of a circle* $= \pi r^2$ ✓ *Circumference of a circle* $= 2\pi r$ r
Example	**Find the area of the circle.** Solution: Use area formula: $Area = \pi r^2$ $r = 2\ in \rightarrow Area = \pi(2)^2 = 4\pi, \pi = 3.14$ **Then:** $Area = 4 \times 3.14 = 12.56\ in^2$ $2\ in$
Your Turn!	**Find the area of each circle.** ($\pi = 3.14$) 1) _____ 5 cm 2) _____ 10 in **Find the Circumference of each circle.** ($\pi = 3.14$) 3) _____ 8 cm 4) _____ 7 m

Find more at

bit.ly/3nJdOP2

Topic	Circles – Answers
Notes	✓ In a circle, variable r is usually used for the radius and d for diameter and π is about 3.14. ✓ *Area of a circle $= \pi r^2$* ✓ *Circumference of a circle $= 2\pi r$* *(diagram of circle with radius r)*

Example	**Find the area of the circle.**
	  Solution:
	  Use area formula: $Area = \pi r^2$
	  $r = 2\ in \rightarrow Area = \pi(2)^2 = 4\pi, \pi = 3.14$
	  Then: $Area = 4 \times 3.14 = 12.56\ in^2$
	
	(diagram of circle with radius 2 in)

Your Turn!

Find the area of each circle. ($\pi = 3.14$)

1) $78.5 cm^2$

(circle with radius 5 cm)

2) $314\ in^2$

(circle with radius 10 in)

Find the Circumference of each circle. ($\pi = 3.14$)

3) $50.24\ cm$

(circle with radius 8 cm)

4) $43.96\ m$

(circle with radius 7 m)

Find more at

bit.ly/3nJdOP2

Topic	Cubes
Notes	✓ A cube is a three-dimensional solid object bounded by six square sides. ✓ Volume is the measure of the amount of space inside of a solid figure, like a cube, ball, cylinder or pyramid. ✓ Volume of a cube $= (one\ side)^3$ ✓ surface area of cube $= 6 \times (one\ side)^2$
Example	**Find the volume and surface area of the following cube.** 15 cm **Solution:** Use volume formula: $volume = (one\ side)^3$ Then: $volume = (one\ side)^3 = (15)^3 = 3,375\ cm^3$ Use surface area formula: $surface\ area\ of\ cube: 6(one\ side)^2 = 6(15)^2 = 6(225) = 1,350\ cm^2$
Your Turn!	**Find the volume of each cube.**

1) _____ 9 in

2) _____ 13 ft

3) _____ 14 cm

4) _____ 20 m

Topic	Cubes – Answers
Notes	✓ A cube is a three-dimensional solid object bounded by six square sides. ✓ Volume is the measure of the amount of space inside of a solid figure, like a cube, ball, cylinder or pyramid. ✓ Volume of a cube $= (one\ side)^3$ ✓ surface area of cube $= 6 \times (one\ side)^2$
Example	***Find the volume and surface area of the following cube.*** $15\ cm$ **Solution:** Use volume formula: $volume = (one\ side)^3$ Then: $volume = (one\ side)^3 = (15)^3 = 3{,}375\ cm^3$ Use surface area formula: $surface\ area\ of\ cube: 6(one\ side)^2 = 6(15)^2 = 6(225) = 1{,}350\ cm^2$
Your Turn! **Find more at** bit.ly/2M6PfOl	***Find the volume of each cube.*** 1) $729\ in^3$ $9\ in$ 2) $2{,}197\ ft^3$ $13\ ft$ 3) $2{,}744\ cm^3$ $14\ cm$ 4) $8{,}000\ m^3$ $20\ m$

Topic	Trapezoids
Notes	✓ A quadrilateral with at least one pair of parallel sides is a trapezoid. ✓ Area of a trapezoid $= \frac{1}{2}h(b_1 + b_2)$
Example	**Calculate the area of the trapezoid.** Solution: Use area formula: $A = \frac{1}{2}h(b_1 + b_2)$ $b_1 = 8\ cm$, $b_2 = 12\ cm$ and $h = 14\ cm$ Then: $A = \frac{1}{2}(14)(12 + 8) = 7(20) = 140\ cm^2$

Your Turn!

1) _____
7 cm, 4 cm, 10 cm

2) _____
8 m, 10 m, 12 m

3) _____
7 ft, 6 ft, 15 ft

4) _____
8 cm, 6 cm, 12 cm

Find more at
bit.ly/3hpKACJ

Topic	Trapezoids – Answers
Notes	✓ A quadrilateral with at least one pair of parallel sides is a trapezoid. ✓ Area of a trapezoid $= \frac{1}{2}h(b_1 + b_2)$
Example	**Calculate the area of the trapezoid.** **Solution:** Use area formula: $A = \frac{1}{2}h(b_1 + b_2)$ $b_1 = 8\ cm$, $b_2 = 12\ cm$ and $h = 14\ cm$ Then: $A = \frac{1}{2}(14)(12 + 8) = 7(20) = 140\ cm^2$

Your Turn!

1) $34\ cm^2$

7 cm
4 cm
10 cm

2) $100\ m^2$

8 m
10 m
12 m

3) $66\ ft^2$

7 ft
6 ft
15 ft

4) $60\ cm^2$

8 cm
6 cm
12 cm

Find more at

bit.ly/3hpKACJ

Topic	**Rectangular Prisms**
Notes	✓ A solid 3-dimensional object which has six rectangular faces. ✓ Volume of a Rectangular prism $= \boldsymbol{Length \times Width \times Height}$ $Volume = l \times w \times h$ $Surface\ area = 2(wh + lw + lh)$
Example	**Find the volume and surface area of rectangular prism.** **Solution:** Use volume formula: $Volume = l \times w \times h$ Then: $Volume = 4 \times 2 \times 6 = 48\ m^3$ Use surface area formula: $Surface\ area = 2(wh + lw + lh)$ Then: $Surface\ area = 2\big((2 \times 6) + (4 \times 2) + (4 \times 6)\big)$ $\qquad\qquad = 2(12 + 8 + 24) = 2(44) = 88\ m^2$
Your Turn!	**Find the surface area of each Rectangular Prism.**

1) _____

5 ft

10 ft

3 ft

2) _____

8 cm

16 cm

6 cm

Find more at

bit.ly/3nKm2GT

3) _____

12 m

18 m

10 m

4) _____

18 in

16 in

12 in

Topic	**Rectangular Prisms - Answers**
Notes	✓ A solid 3-dimensional object which has six rectangular faces. ✓ Volume of a Rectangular prism $= \textbf{Length} \times \textbf{Width} \times \textbf{Height}$ $Volume = l \times w \times h$ $Surface\ area = 2(wh + lw + lh)$
Example	**Find the volume and surface area of rectangular prism.** **Solution:** Use volume formula: $Volume = l \times w \times h$ Then: $Volume = 4 \times 2 \times 6 = 48\ m^3$ Use surface area formula: $Surface\ area = 2(wh + lw + lh)$ Then: $Surface\ area = 2\big((2 \times 6) + (4 \times 2) + (4 \times 6)\big)$ $= 2(12 + 8 + 24) = 2(44) = 88\ m^2$
Your Turn!	**Find the surface area of each Rectangular Prism.**

1) $190\ ft^2$
5 ft, 10 ft, 3 ft

2) $544\ cm^2$
8 cm, 16 cm, 6 cm

3) $1,032\ m^2$
12 m, 18 m, 10 m

4) $1,392\ in^2$
18 in, 16 in, 12 in

Find more at

bit.ly/3nKm2GT

Topic	**Cylinder**
Notes	✓ A cylinder is a solid geometric figure with straight parallel sides and a circular or oval cross section. ✓ *Volume of Cylinder Formula* $= \pi(radius)^2 \times height$ $\pi = 3.14$ ✓ *Surface area of a cylinder* $= 2\pi r^2 + 2\pi rh$
Example	***Find the volume and Surface area of the follow Cylinder.*** Solution: Use volume formula: $Volume = \pi(radius)^2 \times height$ Then: $Volume = \pi(3)^2 \times 12 = 9\pi \times 12 = 108\pi$ $\pi = 3.14$ ***then:*** $Volume = 108\pi = 339.12\ cm^3$ Use surface area formula: $Surface\ area = 2\pi r^2 + 2\pi rh$ ***Then:*** $2\pi(3)^2 + 2\pi(3)(12) = 2\pi(9) + 2\pi(36) = 18\pi + 72\pi = 90\pi$ $\pi = 3.14$ ***Then:*** $Surface\ area = 90 \times 3.14 = 282.6\ cm^2$
Your Turn!	***Find the volume of each Cylinder.*** ($\pi = 3.14$) 1) _____ $8\ in$ $3\ in$ 2) _____ $14\ m$ $5\ m$ ***Find the Surface area of each Cylinder.*** ($\pi = 3.14$) 3) _____ $15\ ft$ $9\ ft$ 4) _____ $12\ cm$ $6\ cm$

Topic	Cylinder – Answers
Notes	✓ A cylinder is a solid geometric figure with straight parallel sides and a circular or oval cross section. ✓ $Volume\ of\ Cylinder\ Formula = \pi(radius)^2 \times height\ \pi = 3.14$ ✓ $Surface\ area\ of\ a\ cylinder = 2\pi r^2 + 2\pi rh$

Example	**Find the volume and Surface area of the follow Cylinder.**
	
	  Solution:
	  Use volume formula: $Volume = \pi(radius)^2 \times height$
	  Then: $Volume = \pi(3)^2 \times 12 = 9\pi \times 12 = 108\pi$
	  $\pi = 3.14$ **then:** $Volume = 108\pi = 339.12\ cm^3$
	  Use surface area formula: $Surface\ area = 2\pi r^2 + 2\pi rh$
	  Then: $2\pi(3)^2 + 2\pi(3)(12) = 2\pi(9) + 2\pi(36) = 18\pi + 72\pi = 90\pi$
	  $\pi = 3.14$ **Then:** $Surface\ area = 90 \times 3.14 = 282.6\ cm^2$
	12 cm 3 cm

Your Turn!	**Find the volume of each Cylinder.** ($\pi = 3.14$)

1) $226.08\ in^3$ 8 in 3 in	2) $1,099\ m^3$ 14 m 5 m

Find the Surface area of each Cylinder. ($\pi = 3.14$)

3) $1,356.48\ ft^2$ 15 ft 9 ft	4) $678.24\ cm^2$ 12 cm 6 cm

Find more at

bit.ly/37LtcVM

Topic	Mean, Median, Mode, and Range of the Given Data
Notes	✓ Mean: $\dfrac{sum\ of\ the\ data}{total\ number\ of\ data\ entires}$ ✓ Mode: value in the list that appears most often. ✓ Median: is the middle number of a group of numbers that have been arranged in order by size. ✓ Range: the difference of largest value and smallest value in the list.
Example	***Find the mode and median of these numbers?*** $16, 10, 6, 3, 1, 16, 2, 4$ **Solution:** Mode: value in the list that appears most often. Number 16 is the value in the list that appears most often (there are two number 16). To find median, write the numbers in order: $1, 2, 3, 4, 6, 10, 16, 16$ Number 4 and 6 are in the middle. Find their average: $\dfrac{4+6}{2} = \dfrac{10}{2} = 5$ The median is 5.

Your Turn!		
	1) $5, 2, 4, 8, 5, 6$ Mode: _____ Range: _____ Mean: _____ Median: _____	2) $6, 3, 2, 9, 5, 7, 2, 14$ Mode: _____ Range: _____ Mean: _____ Median: _____
Find more at bit.ly/2KO86gg	3) $5, 4, 3, 2, 9, 5, 6, 8, 12$ Mode: _____ Range: _____ Mean: _____ Median: _____	4) $10, 3, 8, 3, 9, 3, 4, 14$ Mode: _____ Range: _____ Mean: _____ Median: _____

Topic	Mean, Median, Mode, and Range of the Given Data - Answers
Notes	✓ Mean: $\dfrac{sum\ of\ the\ data}{total\ number\ of\ data\ entires}$ ✓ Mode: value in the list that appears most often. ✓ Median: is the middle number of a group of numbers that have been arranged in order by size. ✓ Range: the difference of largest value and smallest value in the list.
Example	**Find the mode and median of these numbers?** $16, 10, 6, 3, 1, 16, 2, 4$ **Solution:** Mode: value in the list that appears most often. Number 16 is the value in the list that appears most often (there are two number 16). To find median, write the numbers in order: $1, 2, 3, 4, 6, 10, 16, 16$ Number 4 and 6 are in the middle. Find their average: $\dfrac{4+6}{2} = \dfrac{10}{2} = 5$ The median is 5.

Your Turn!	1) $5, 2, 4, 8, 5, 6$	2) $6, 3, 2, 9, 5, 7, 2, 14$
	Mode: 5 Range: 6	Mode: 2 Range: 12
	Mean: 5 Median: 5	Mean: 6 Median: 5.5
Find more at bit.ly/2KO86gg	3) $5, 4, 3, 2, 9, 5, 6, 8, 12$	4) $10, 3, 8, 3, 9, 3, 4, 14$
	Mode: 5 Range: 10	Mode: 3 Range: 11
	Mean: 6 Median: 5	Mean: 6.75 Median: 6

Topic	Probability Problems
Notes	✓ Probability is the likelihood of something happening in the future. It is expressed as a number between zero (can never happen) to 1 (will always happen). ✓ Probability can be expressed as a fraction, a decimal, or a percent. ✓ Probability formula: $Probability = \frac{number\ of\ desired\ outcomes}{number\ of\ total\ outcomes}$
Example	*If there are 3 green balls, 4 red balls, and 10 blue balls in a basket, what is the probability that Jason will pick out a red ball from the basket?* **Solution:** There are 4 red ball and 17 are total number of balls. Therefore, probability that Jason will pick out a red ball from the basket is 4 out of 17 or $\frac{4}{3+4+10} = \frac{4}{17}$
Your Turn! **Find more at** bit.ly/3phwk1p	1) A number is chosen at random from 1 to 15. Find the probability of selecting a prime number. (A prime number is a whole number that is only divisible by itself and 1) _____ 2) There are only red and blue cards in a box. The probability of choosing a red card in the box at random is one third. If there are 24 blue cards, how many cards are in the box? _____ 3) A die is rolled, what is the probability that an odd number is obtained? _____

Topic	Probability Problems – Answers
Notes	✓ Probability is the likelihood of something happening in the future. It is expressed as a number between zero (can never happen) to 1 (will always happen). ✓ Probability can be expressed as a fraction, a decimal, or a percent. ✓ Probability formula: $Probability = \dfrac{number\ of\ desired\ outcomes}{number\ of\ total\ outcomes}$
Example	***If there are 3 green balls, 4 red balls, and 10 blue balls in a basket, what is the probability that Jason will pick out a red ball from the basket?*** **Solution:** There are 4 red ball and 17 are total number of balls. Therefore, probability that Jason will pick out a red ball from the basket is 4 out of 17 or $\dfrac{4}{3+4+10} = \dfrac{4}{17}$
Your Turn! **Find more at** bit.ly/3phwk1p	1) A number is chosen at random from 1 to 15. Find the probability of selecting a prime number. (A prime number is a whole number that is only divisible by itself and 1) $\frac{6}{15} = \frac{2}{5}$ *(There are 6 prime numbers from 1 to 15: 2, 3, 5, 7, 11, 13)*
	2) There are only red and blue cards in a box. The probability of choosing a red card in the box at random is one third. If there are 24 blue cards, how many cards are in the box? 36
	3) A die is rolled, what is the probability that an odd number is obtained? $\frac{1}{2}$

Topic	Pie Graph
Notes	✓ A Pie Chart is a circle chart divided into sectors, each sector represents the relative size of each value.
Example	A library has 460 books that include Mathematics, Physics, Chemistry, English and History. Use following graph to answer the question. **What is the number of Physics books?** **Solution:** Number of total books $= 460$ Percent of Physics books $= 25\% = 0.25$ Then, umber of Physics books: $$0.25 \times 460 = 115$$ History 10%, Mathematics 30%, English 15%, Chemistry 20%, Physics 25%
Your Turn! **Find more at** bit.ly/34ECTDv	The circle graph below shows all Mr. Smith's expenses for last month. Mr. Smith spent \$400 for clothes last month. Foods 25%, Bills 20%, Others 23%, Clothes 20%, Books 12% Mr. Smith's last month expenses 1) How much did Mr. Smith spend for his Books last month? _____ 2) How much did Mr. Smith spend for Bills last month? _____ 3) How much did Mr. Smith spend for his foods last month? _____

Topic	Pie Graph
Notes	✓ A Pie Chart is a circle chart divided into sectors, each sector represents the relative size of each value.

| **Example** | A library has 460 books that include Mathematics, Physics, Chemistry, English and History. Use following graph to answer the question.

 What is the number of Physics books?
 Solution: Number of total books $= 460$
 Percent of Physics books $= 25\% = 0.25$
 Then, umber of Physics books:
 $$0.25 \times 460 = 115$$

 |

Your Turn!	The circle graph below shows all Mr. Smith's expenses for last month. Mr. Smith spent $400 for clothes last month. Mr. Smith's last month expenses
Find more at bit.ly/34ECTDv [QR code]	1) How much did Mr. Smith spend for his Books last month? $240 2) How much did Mr. Smith spend for Bills last month? $400 3) How much did Mr. Smith spend for his foods last month? $500

Topic	Permutations and Combinations
Notes	✓ Permutations: The number of ways to choose a sample of k elements from a set of n distinct objects where order does matter, and replacements are not allowed. For a permutation problem, use this formula: $$_nP_k = \frac{n!}{(n-k)!}$$ ✓ Combination: The number of ways to choose a sample of r elements from a set of n distinct objects where order does not matter, and replacements are not allowed. For a combination problem, use this formula: $$_nC_r = \frac{n!}{r!\,(n-r)!}$$ ✓ Factorials are products, indicated by an exclamation mark. For example, 4! Equals: $4 \times 3 \times 2 \times 1$. Remember that 0! is defined to be equal to 1.
Example	*How many ways can we pick a team of 4 people from a group of 8?* **Solution:** Since the order doesn't matter, we need to use combination formula where n is 8 and r is 4. Then: $\frac{n!}{r!\,(n-r)!} = \frac{8!}{4!\,(8-4)!} = \frac{8!}{4!\,(4)!} = \frac{8\times7\times6\times5\times4!}{4!\,(4)!} = \frac{8\times7\times6\times5}{4\times3\times2\times1} = \frac{1,680}{24} = 70$
Your Turn!	1) In how many ways can 6 athletes be arranged in a straight line? _____
	2) How many ways can we award a first and second place prize among eight contestants? _____
Find more at bit.ly/34BQgUY	3) In how many ways can we choose 4 players from a team of 10 players? _____

Topic	Permutations and Combinations – Answers
Notes	✓ Permutations: The number of ways to choose a sample of k elements from a set of n distinct objects where order does matter, and replacements are not allowed. For a permutation problem, use this formula: $$_nP_k = \frac{n!}{(n-k)!}$$ ✓ Combination: The number of ways to choose a sample of r elements from a set of n distinct objects where order does not matter, and replacements are not allowed. For a combination problem, use this formula: $$_nC_r = \frac{n!}{r!\,(n-r)!}$$ ✓ Factorials are products, indicated by an exclamation mark. For example, 4! Equals: $4 \times 3 \times 2 \times 1$. Remember that 0! is defined to be equal to 1.
Example	***How many ways can we pick a team of 4 people from a group of 8?*** **Solution:** Since the order doesn't matter, we need to use combination formula where n is 8 and r is 4. Then: $\frac{n!}{r!\,(n-r)!} = \frac{8!}{4!\,(8-4)!} = \frac{8!}{4!\,(4)!} = \frac{8\times7\times6\times5\times4!}{4!\,(4)!} = \frac{8\times7\times6\times5}{4\times3\times2\times1} = \frac{1,680}{24} = 70$
Your Turn! **Find more at** bit.ly/34BQgUY	1) In how many ways can 6 athletes be arranged in a straight line? 720
	2) How many ways can we award a first and second place prize among eight contestants? 56
	3) In how many ways can we choose 4 players from a team of 10 players? 210

Topic	Function Notation and Evaluation
Notes	✓ Functions are mathematical operations that assign unique outputs to given inputs. ✓ Function notation is the way a function is written. It is meant to be a precise way of giving information about the function without a rather lengthy written explanation. ✓ The most popular function notation is $f(x)$ which is read "f of x". ✓ To evaluate a function, plug in the input (the given value or expression) for the function's variable (place holder, x).
Example	**Evaluate**: $h(n) = 2n^2 - 2$, find $h(2)$. **Solution:** Substitute n with 2: Then: $h(n) = 2n^2 - 2 \rightarrow h(2) = 2(2)^2 - 2 = 8 - 2 \rightarrow h(2) = 6$

Your Turn!	1) $f(x) = x - 1$, find $f(-2)$ _____	2) $g(x) = 3x + 2$, find $g(2)$ _____
	3) $g(n) = 2n - 8$, find $g(-1)$ _____	4) $h(n) = n^2 - 1$, find $h(-2)$ _____
	5) $f(x) = x^2 + 12$, find $f(5)$ _____	6) $g(x) = 2x^2 - 9$, find $g(-2)$_____
Find more at bit.ly/3mIs7lF	7) $w(x) = 3x^2 - x$, find $w(2n)$ _____	8) $p(x) = 2x^3 - 8$, find $p(-2a)$ _____

Topic	Function Notation and Evaluation – Answers
Notes	✓ Functions are mathematical operations that assign unique outputs to given inputs. ✓ Function notation is the way a function is written. It is meant to be a precise way of giving information about the function without a rather lengthy written explanation. ✓ The most popular function notation is $f(x)$ which is read "f of x". ✓ To evaluate a function, plug in the input (the given value or expression) for the function's variable (place holder, x).
Example	**Evaluate**: $h(n) = 2n^2 - 2$, find $h(2)$. **Solution:** Substitute n with 2: Then: $h(n) = 2n^2 - 2 \rightarrow h(2) = 2(2)^2 - 2 = 8 - 2 \rightarrow h(2) = 6$

Your Turn!

1) $f(x) = x - 1$, find $f(-2)$ $f(-2) = -3$	2) $g(x) = 3x + 2$, find $g(2)$ $g(2) = 8$
3) $g(n) = 2n - 8$, find $g(-1)$ $g(-1) = -10$	4) $h(n) = n^2 - 1$, find $h(-2)$ $h(-2) = 3$
5) $f(x) = x^2 + 12$, find $f(5)$ $f(5) = 37$	6) $g(x) = 2x^2 - 9$, find $g(-2)$ $g(-2) = -1$
7) $w(x) = 3x^2 - x$, find $w(2n)$ $w(3n) = 12n^2 - 2n$	8) $p(x) = 2x^3 - 8$, find $p(-2a)$ $p(-2a) = -16a^3 - 8$

Find more at

bit.ly/3mIs7lF

Topic	Adding and Subtracting Functions
Notes	✓ Just like we can add and subtract numbers and expressions, we can add or subtract two functions and simplify or evaluate them. The result is a new function. ✓ For two functions $f(x)$ and $g(x)$, we can create two new functions: $(f+g)(x) = f(x) + g(x)$ and $(f-g)(x) = f(x) - g(x)$
Example	$g(a) = 2a - 5$, $f(a) = a + 8$, **Find:** $(g+f)(a)$ **Solution:** $(g+f)(a) = g(a) + f(a)$ Then: $(g+f)(a) = (2a - 5) + (a + 8) = 3a + 3$

Your Turn!		
	1) $g(x) = x - 3$ $h(x) = 2x + 5$ Find: $(h+g)(2)$ _____	2) $f(x) = 2x + 6$ $g(x) = -x - 5$ Find: $(f+g)(3)$ _____
	3) $f(x) = 5x + 8$ $g(x) = 3x - 12$ Find: $(f-g)(-2)$ _____	4) $h(x) = 2x^2 - 10$ $g(x) = 3x + 12$ Find: $(h+g)(3)$ _____
Find more at bit.ly/3hdeFVO	5) $g(x) = 10x - 7$ $h(x) = 3x^2 + 11$ Find: $(h-g)(x)$ _____	6) $h(x) = -x^2 - 15$ $g(x) = 3x^2 + 18$ Find: $(h-g)(a)$ _____

Topic	Adding and Subtracting Functions – Answers
Notes	✓ Just like we can add and subtract numbers and expressions, we can add or subtract two functions and simplify or evaluate them. The result is a new function. ✓ For two functions $f(x)$ and $g(x)$, we can create two new functions: $(f + g)(x) = f(x) + g(x)$ and $(f - g)(x) = f(x) - g(x)$
Example	$g(a) = 2a - 5, f(a) = a + 8$, Find: $(g + f)(a)$ **Solution:** $(g + f)(a) = g(a) + f(a)$ Then: $(g + f)(a) = (2a - 5) + (a + 8) = 3a + 3$

Your Turn!		
	1) $g(x) = x - 3$ $h(x) = 2x + 5$ Find: $(h + g)(2)$ 8	2) $f(x) = 2x + 6$ $g(x) = -x - 5$ Find: $(f + g)(3)$ 4
	3) $f(x) = 5x + 8$ $g(x) = 3x - 12$ Find: $(f - g)(-2)$ 16	4) $h(x) = 2x^2 - 10$ $g(x) = 3x + 12$ Find: $(h + g)(3)$ 29
Find more at bit.ly/3hdeFVO	5) $g(x) = 10x - 7$ $h(x) = 3x^2 + 11$ Find: $(h - g)(x)$ $3x^2 - 10x + 18$	6) $h(x) = -x^2 - 15$ $g(x) = 3x^2 + 18$ Find: $(h - g)(a)$ $-4a^2 - 33$

Topic	Multiplying and Dividing Functions
Notes	✓ Just like we can multiply and divide numbers and expressions, we can multiply and divide two functions and simplify or evaluate them. ✓ For two functions $f(x)$ and $g(x)$, we can create two new functions: $(f.g)(x) = f(x).g(x)$ and $\left(\dfrac{f}{g}\right)(x) = \dfrac{f(x)}{g(x)}$
Example	$g(x) = x + 5, f(x) = x - 3$, Find: $(g.f)(2)$ **Solution:** $(g.f)(x) = g(x).f(x) = (x + 5)(x - 3) = x^2 - 3x + 5x - 15 = x^2 + 2x - 15$ Substitute x with 2: $(g.f)(x) = (2)^2 + 2(2) - 15 = 4 + 4 - 15 = -7$

Your Turn!

1) $g(x) = x - 1$

   $h(x) = x + 2$

   Find: $(g.h)(-3)$

   _____

2) $f(x) = x + 2$

   $g(x) = -x - 3$

   Find: $\left(\dfrac{f}{g}\right)(-4)$

   _____

3) $f(x) = 5x + 3$

   $g(x) = 2x - 4$

   Find: $\left(\dfrac{f}{g}\right)(5)$

   _____

4) $h(x) = x^2 - 2$

   $g(x) = x + 4$

   Find: $(g.h)(3)$

   _____

Find more at

bit.ly/3ph7kHA

5) $g(x) = 2x - 8$

   $h(x) = x^2 + 6$

   Find: $(g.h)(-2)$

   _____

6) $h(x) = 3x^2 - 8$

   $g(x) = 4x + 3$

   Find: $\left(\dfrac{h}{g}\right)(-1)$

   _____

Topic	Multiplying and Dividing Functions - Answers
Notes	✓ Just like we can multiply and divide numbers and expressions, we can multiply and divide two functions and simplify or evaluate them. ✓ For two functions $f(x)$ and $g(x)$, we can create two new functions: $(f.g)(x) = f(x).g(x)$ and $\left(\frac{f}{g}\right)(x) = \frac{f(x)}{g(x)}$
Example	$g(x) = x + 5, f(x) = x - 3$, Find: $(g.f)(2)$ **Solution:** $(g.f)(x) = g(x).f(x) = (x + 5)(x - 3) = x^2 - 3x + 5x - 15 = x^2 + 2x - 15$ Substitute x with 2: $(g.f)(x) = (2)^2 + 2(2) - 15 = 4 + 4 - 15 = -7$

Your Turn!	1) $g(x) = x - 1$ $h(x) = x + 2$ Find: $(g.h)(-3)$ $(g.h)(-3) = 4$	2) $f(x) = x + 2$ $g(x) = -x - 3$ Find: $\left(\frac{f}{g}\right)(-4)$ $\left(\frac{f}{g}\right)(-4) = -2$
	3) $f(x) = 5x + 3$ $g(x) = 2x - 4$ Find: $\left(\frac{f}{g}\right)(5)$ $\left(\frac{f}{g}\right)(5) = \frac{14}{3}$	4) $h(x) = x^2 - 2$ $g(x) = x + 4$ Find: $(g.h)(3)$ $(g.h)(3) = 49$
Find more at bit.ly/3ph7kHA	5) $g(x) = 2x - 8$ $h(x) = x^2 + 6$ Find: $(g.h)(-2)$ $(g.h)(-2) = -120$	6) $h(x) = 3x^2 - 8$ $g(x) = 4x + 3$ Find: $\left(\frac{h}{g}\right)(-1)$ $\left(\frac{h}{g}\right)(-1) = 5$

Time to test

Time to refine your quantitative reasoning skill with a practice test

In this section, there are two complete ISEE Upper Level Mathematics practice tests. Take these tests to simulate the test day experience. After you've finished, score your tests using the answer keys.

Before You Start

- You'll need a pencil and a timer to take the test.

- It's okay to guess. There is no penalty for wrong answers.

- After you've finished the test, review the answer key to see where you went wrong.

- After you've finished the test, review the answer key to see where you went wrong.

- For each multiple-choice question, there are four possible answers. Choose which one is best. For grids in questions, write your answer in the answer boxes at the top of the grid. Then, as shown below fill in a bubble under each box in which you wrote your answer.

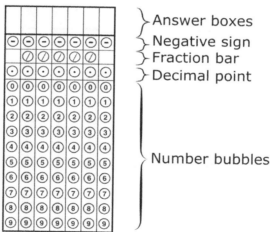

Good Luck!

ISEE Upper Level Mathematics

Practice Test 1

2022-2023

Two Parts

Total number of questions: 84

Part 1 (Calculator): 37 questions

Part 2 (Calculator): 47 questions

Total time for two parts: 75 Minutes

139

ISEE Upper Level Practice Tests Answer Sheet

Remove (or photocopy) these answer sheets and use them to complete the practice tests.

ISEE Upper Level Practice Test 1

Quantitative Reasoning

1 Ⓐ Ⓑ Ⓒ Ⓓ	25 Ⓐ Ⓑ Ⓒ Ⓓ		
2 Ⓐ Ⓑ Ⓒ Ⓓ	26 Ⓐ Ⓑ Ⓒ Ⓓ		
3 Ⓐ Ⓑ Ⓒ Ⓓ	27 Ⓐ Ⓑ Ⓒ Ⓓ		
4 Ⓐ Ⓑ Ⓒ Ⓓ	28 Ⓐ Ⓑ Ⓒ Ⓓ		
5 Ⓐ Ⓑ Ⓒ Ⓓ	29 Ⓐ Ⓑ Ⓒ Ⓓ		
6 Ⓐ Ⓑ Ⓒ Ⓓ	30 Ⓐ Ⓑ Ⓒ Ⓓ		
7 Ⓐ Ⓑ Ⓒ Ⓓ	31 Ⓐ Ⓑ Ⓒ Ⓓ		
8 Ⓐ Ⓑ Ⓒ Ⓓ	32 Ⓐ Ⓑ Ⓒ Ⓓ		
9 Ⓐ Ⓑ Ⓒ Ⓓ	33 Ⓐ Ⓑ Ⓒ Ⓓ		
10 Ⓐ Ⓑ Ⓒ Ⓓ	34 Ⓐ Ⓑ Ⓒ Ⓓ		
11 Ⓐ Ⓑ Ⓒ Ⓓ	35 Ⓐ Ⓑ Ⓒ Ⓓ		
12 Ⓐ Ⓑ Ⓒ Ⓓ	36 Ⓐ Ⓑ Ⓒ Ⓓ		
13 Ⓐ Ⓑ Ⓒ Ⓓ	37 Ⓐ Ⓑ Ⓒ Ⓓ		
14 Ⓐ Ⓑ Ⓒ Ⓓ			
15 Ⓐ Ⓑ Ⓒ Ⓓ			
16 Ⓐ Ⓑ Ⓒ Ⓓ			
17 Ⓐ Ⓑ Ⓒ Ⓓ			
18 Ⓐ Ⓑ Ⓒ Ⓓ			
19 Ⓐ Ⓑ Ⓒ Ⓓ			
20 Ⓐ Ⓑ Ⓒ Ⓓ			
21 Ⓐ Ⓑ Ⓒ Ⓓ			
22 Ⓐ Ⓑ Ⓒ Ⓓ			
23 Ⓐ Ⓑ Ⓒ Ⓓ			
24 Ⓐ Ⓑ Ⓒ Ⓓ			

Mathematics Achievement

1 Ⓐ Ⓑ Ⓒ Ⓓ	25 Ⓐ Ⓑ Ⓒ Ⓓ
2 Ⓐ Ⓑ Ⓒ Ⓓ	26 Ⓐ Ⓑ Ⓒ Ⓓ
3 Ⓐ Ⓑ Ⓒ Ⓓ	27 Ⓐ Ⓑ Ⓒ Ⓓ
4 Ⓐ Ⓑ Ⓒ Ⓓ	28 Ⓐ Ⓑ Ⓒ Ⓓ
5 Ⓐ Ⓑ Ⓒ Ⓓ	29 Ⓐ Ⓑ Ⓒ Ⓓ
6 Ⓐ Ⓑ Ⓒ Ⓓ	30 Ⓐ Ⓑ Ⓒ Ⓓ
7 Ⓐ Ⓑ Ⓒ Ⓓ	31 Ⓐ Ⓑ Ⓒ Ⓓ
8 Ⓐ Ⓑ Ⓒ Ⓓ	32 Ⓐ Ⓑ Ⓒ Ⓓ
9 Ⓐ Ⓑ Ⓒ Ⓓ	33 Ⓐ Ⓑ Ⓒ Ⓓ
10 Ⓐ Ⓑ Ⓒ Ⓓ	34 Ⓐ Ⓑ Ⓒ Ⓓ
11 Ⓐ Ⓑ Ⓒ Ⓓ	35 Ⓐ Ⓑ Ⓒ Ⓓ
12 Ⓐ Ⓑ Ⓒ Ⓓ	36 Ⓐ Ⓑ Ⓒ Ⓓ
13 Ⓐ Ⓑ Ⓒ Ⓓ	37 Ⓐ Ⓑ Ⓒ Ⓓ
14 Ⓐ Ⓑ Ⓒ Ⓓ	38 Ⓐ Ⓑ Ⓒ Ⓓ
15 Ⓐ Ⓑ Ⓒ Ⓓ	39 Ⓐ Ⓑ Ⓒ Ⓓ
16 Ⓐ Ⓑ Ⓒ Ⓓ	40 Ⓐ Ⓑ Ⓒ Ⓓ
17 Ⓐ Ⓑ Ⓒ Ⓓ	41 Ⓐ Ⓑ Ⓒ Ⓓ
18 Ⓐ Ⓑ Ⓒ Ⓓ	42 Ⓐ Ⓑ Ⓒ Ⓓ
19 Ⓐ Ⓑ Ⓒ Ⓓ	43 Ⓐ Ⓑ Ⓒ Ⓓ
20 Ⓐ Ⓑ Ⓒ Ⓓ	44 Ⓐ Ⓑ Ⓒ Ⓓ
21 Ⓐ Ⓑ Ⓒ Ⓓ	45 Ⓐ Ⓑ Ⓒ Ⓓ
22 Ⓐ Ⓑ Ⓒ Ⓓ	46 Ⓐ Ⓑ Ⓒ Ⓓ
23 Ⓐ Ⓑ Ⓒ Ⓓ	47 Ⓐ Ⓑ Ⓒ Ⓓ
24 Ⓐ Ⓑ Ⓒ Ⓓ	

ISEE Upper Level

Practice Test 1

Part 1 (Quantitative Reasoning)

37 questions

Total time for this section: 35 Minutes

You may NOT use a calculator for this test.

1) How much greater is the value of $4x + 9$ than the value of $4x - 3$?

A. 8

B. 10

C. 12

D. 14

2) What is the prime factorization of 1,400?

A. $2 \times 2 \times 5 \times 5$

B. $2 \times 2 \times 2 \times 5 \times 5 \times 7$

C. 2×5

D. $2 \times 2 \times 2 \times 5 \times 7$

3) If 6 inches on a map represents an actual distance of 150 feet, then what actual distance does 20 inches on the map represent?

A. 180 feet

B. 200 feet

C. 250 feet

D. 500 feet

4) The circle graph below shows all Mr. Green's expenses for last month. If he spent $550 on his car, how much did he spend for his rent?

A. $675

B. $750

C. $780

D. $810

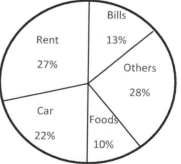

Mr. Green's monthly expenses

5) The area of a circle is less than 49π. Which of the following can be the circumference of the circle?

A. 10π

B. 14π

C. 24π

D. 32π

6) A basket contains 25 balls and the average weight of each of these balls is 35 g. The five heaviest balls have an average weight of 50 g each. If we remove the three heaviest balls from the basket, what is the average weight of the remaining balls?

A. 10 g

B. 20.25 g

C. 31.25 g

D. 35 g

7) If $f(x) = x^2 + 6$, what is the smallest possible value of $f(x)$?

A. 0

B. 5

C. 6

D. 7

8) Alice drives from her house to work at an average speed of 45 miles per hour and she drives at an average speed of 65 miles per hour when she was returning home. What was her minimum speed on the round trip in miles per hour?

A. 45

B. 58.5

C. 65

D. Cannot be determined

9) If the sum of the positive integers from 1 to n is 3,350, and the sum of the positive integers from $n + 1$ to $2n$ is 4,866, which of the following represents the sum of the positive integers from 1 to $2n$ inclusive?

A. 3,350

B. 4,866

C. 7,000

D. 8,216

10) Oscar purchased a new hat that was on sale for $8.34. The original price was $14.65. What percentage discount was the sale price?

A. 4.2%

B. 40.5%

C. 43%

D. 45%

11) Which of the following statements is correct, according to the graph below?

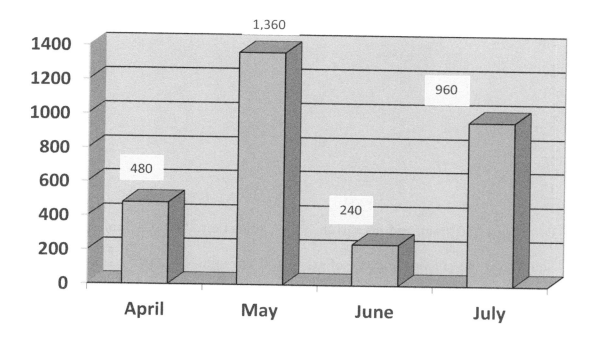

Number of Books Sold in a Bookstore

A. Number of books sold in April was twice the number of books sold in July.

B. Number of books sold in July was less than half the number of books sold in May.

C. Number of books sold in June was half the number of books sold in April.

D. Number of books sold in July was equal to the number of books sold in April plus the number of books sold in June.

12) List A consists of the numbers $\{2, 4, 9, 11, 16\}$, and list B consists of the numbers $\{5, 7, 13, 15, 18\}$.

If the two lists are combined, what is the median of the combined list?

A. 7

B. 8

C. 9

D. 10

13) A bag contains 19 balls: three green, five black, eight blue, a brown, a red and one white. If 17 balls are removed from the bag at random, what is the probability that a brown ball has been removed?

A. $\dfrac{1}{9}$

B. $\dfrac{1}{6}$

C. $\dfrac{16}{19}$

D. $\dfrac{17}{19}$

14) If Jim adds 150 stamps to his current stamp collection, the total number of stamps will be equal to $\dfrac{4}{3}$ the current number of stamps. If Jim adds 40% more stamps to the current collection, how many stamps will be in the collection?

A. 340

B. 453

C. 512

D. 630

15) If $x + y = 7$ and $x - y = 6$ then what is the value of $(x^2 - y^2)$?

A. 24

B. 42

C. 65

D. 90

16) The area of rectangle $ABCD$ is 108 square inches. If the length of the rectangle is three times the width, what is the perimeter of rectangle $ABCD$?

A. 48 inches

B. 67 inches

C. 76 inches

D. 86 inches

17) What's The ratio of boys and girls in a class is $7:4$. If there are 55 students in the class, how many more girls should be enrolled to make the ratio $1:1$?

A. 6

B. 10

C. 12

D. 15

18) The sum of 8 numbers is greater than 320 and less than 480. Which of the following could be the average (arithmetic mean) of the numbers?

A. 30

B. 35

C. 40

D. 45

19) A gas tank can hold 35 gallons when it is $\frac{5}{2}$ full. How many gallons does it contain when it is full?

A. 125

B. 62.5

C. 50

D. 14

20) Triangle ABC is similar to triangle ∠

A. 4

B. 10

C. 18

D. 45

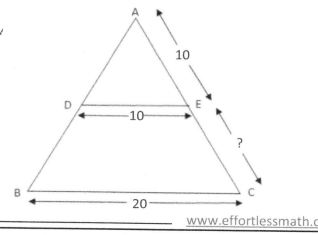

21) Which of the following expressions gives the value of b in terms of f, c, and z from the following equation?

$$f = [\frac{cz}{b}]^2$$

A. $b = fc^2z^2$

B. $b = \frac{cz}{\sqrt{f}}$

C. $b = \frac{\sqrt{f}}{cz}$

D. $b = [\frac{cz}{f}]^2$

Quantitative Comparisons

Direction: Questions 22 to 37 are Quantitative Comparisons Questions. Using the information provided in each question, compare the quantity in column A to the quantity in Column B. Choose on your answer sheet grid

A   if the quantity in Column A is greater

B   if the quantity in Column B is greater

C   if the two quantities are equal

D   if the relationship cannot be determined from the information given

22)

Column A	Column B
5^2	$\sqrt[3]{125}$

23)

Column A	Column B
7	$(52)^{\frac{1}{2}}$

24)

Column A	Column B
The average of $21, 29$, and 37	28

25)

Column A	Column B
$16 \times 435 \times 25$	$19 \times 435 \times 22$

26) x is an integer

Column A	Column B
$-x$	$\dfrac{x}{3}$

27)

Column A	Column B
$(\dfrac{1}{4})^3$	4^{-3}

28) $3x + 7 > x - 1$

Column A	Column B
x	-7

29)

Column A	Column B
The greatest value of x in	The greatest value of x in
$8\,\lvert 3x - 2\rvert = 16$	$8\,\lvert 3x - 2\rvert = 16$

30) x is an integer

Column A	Column B
$(x)^5(x)^2$	$(x^5)^2$

31)

Column A	Column B
The probability that	The probability that
event x will occur.	event x will not occur.

32) The selling price of a sport jacket including 20% discount is $68.

Column A	Column B
Original price of the sport jacket	$80

33) $x^2 - 2x - 20 = 15$

Column A	Column B
x	5

34)

Column A	Column B
$(0.82)^{28}$	$(0.82)^{27}$

35)

Column A	Column B
The probability of rolling a 4 on a die and getting heads on a coin toss.	The probability of rolling an odd number on a die and picking a spade from a deck of 52 cards.

36)

Column A	Column B
$0.46	Sum of one quarter, three nickels, and three pennies

37) x is an odd integer, and y is an even integer. In a certain game an odd number is considered greater than an even number.

Column A	Column B
$x(x + y)$	$(x - y) - y^2$

ISEE Upper Level

Practice Test 1

Part 2 (Mathematics Achievement)

47 questions

Total time for this section: 40 Minutes

You may NOT use a calculator for this test.

1) Which of the following points lies on the line $4x + 6y = 20$?

   A. $(2, 1)$

   B. $(-1, 3)$

   C. $(-2, 2)$

   D. $(2, 2)$

2) 5 less than twice a positive integer is 91. What is the integer?

   A. 40

   B. 41

   C. 42

   D. 48

3) If $\dfrac{|3+x|}{5} \leq 8$, then which of the following is correct?

   A. $-43 \leq x \leq 37$

   B. $-43 \leq x \leq 32$

   C. $-32 \leq x \leq 38$

   D. $-32 \leq x \leq 32$

4) $\dfrac{1}{5b^2} + \dfrac{1}{5b} = \dfrac{1}{b^2}$, then $=$?

   A. $-\dfrac{16}{5}$

   B. 4

   C. $-\dfrac{5}{16}$

   D. 8

5) An angle is equal to one ninth of its supplement. What is the measure of that angle?

   A. $18°$

   B. $40°$

   C. $60°$

   D. $80°$

6) 1.3 is what percent of 26?

   A. 1.3

   B. 5

   C. 18

   D. 24

7) The cost, in thousands of dollars, of producing x thousands of textbooks is

   $C(x) = x^2 + 2x$. The revenue, also in thousands of dollars, is $R(x) = 40x$. find the profit or

   loss if 20 textbooks are produced. ($profit = revenue - cost$)

   A. $2,160 profit

   B. $360 profit

   C. $2,160 loss

   D. $360 loss

8) Simplify $7x^3y^3(2x^3y)^3 =$

   A. $14x^4y^6$

   B. $14x^8y^6$

   C. $56x^{12}y^6$

   D. $56x^8y^6$

9) Ella (E) is 5 years older than her friend Ava (A) who is 4 years younger than her sister Sofia

   (S). If E, A and S denote their ages, which one of the following represents the given

   information?

   A. $\begin{cases} E = A + 5 \\ S = A - 4 \end{cases}$

   B. $\begin{cases} E = A + 5 \\ A = S + 4 \end{cases}$

   C. $\begin{cases} A = E + 5 \\ S = A - 4 \end{cases}$

   D. $\begin{cases} E = A + 5 \\ A = S - 4 \end{cases}$

10) Right triangle ABC has two legs of lengths $4\ cm\ (AB)$ and $3\ cm\ (AC)$. What is the length of the third side (BC)?

    A. $5\ cm$

    B. $6\ cm$

    C. $9\ cm$

    D. $10\ cm$

11) Which is the longest time?

    A. $24\ hours$

    B. $1,520\ minutes$

    C. $3\ days$

    D. $4,200\ seconds$

12) A circle has a diameter of 10 inches. What is its approximate circumference?

    A. 6.28 inches.

    B. 25.12 inches.

    C. 31.4 inches.

    D. 35.12 inches.

13) Write 623 in expanded form, using exponents.

    A. $(6 \times 10^3) + (2 \times 10^2) + (3 \times 10)$

    B. $(6 \times 10^2) + (2 \times 10^1) - 5$

    C. $(6 \times 10^2) + (2 \times 10^1) + 3$

    D. $(6 \times 10^1) + (2 \times 10^2) + 3$

14) What is the area of an isosceles right triangle with hypotenuse that measures $8\ cm$?

    A. $9\ cm^2$

    B. $16\ cm^2$

    C. $3\sqrt{2}\ cm^2$

    D. $64\ cm^2$

15) A company pays its writer $5 for every 500 words written. How much will a writer earn for an article with 860 words?

   A. $12

   B. $5.6

   C. $8.6

   D. $10.7

16) A circular logo is enlarged to fit the lid of a jar. The new diameter is 20% larger than the original. By what percentage has the area of the logo increased?

   A. 20%

   B. 44%

   C. 69%

   D. 75%

17) $89.44 \div 0.05 = ?$

   A. 17.888

   B. 1,788.8

   C. 178.88

   D. 1.7888

18) What's the area of the non-shaded part of the following figure?

   A. 225

   B. 152

   C. 40

   D. 42

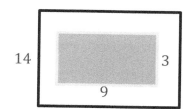

19) A bread recipe calls for $2\frac{1}{2}$ cups of flour. If you only have $1\frac{5}{4}$ cups, how much more flour is needed?

   A. 1

   B. $\frac{1}{2}$

   C. 2

   D. $\frac{1}{4}$

20) What is the maximum value for y if $y = -(x-2)^2 + 7$?

A. -7

B. -2

C. 2

D. 7

21) What is the solution of the following system of equations?

$$\begin{cases} -3x - y = -5 \\ 5x - 5y = 15 \end{cases}$$

A. $(-1, 2)$

B. $(2, -1)$

C. $(1, 4)$

D. $(4, -2)$

22) The equation of a line is given as: $y = 5x - 3$. Which of the following points does not lie on the line?

A. $(2, 7)$

B. $(-2, -13)$

C. $(4, 21)$

D. $(-4, -23)$

23) The drivers at $G \& G$ trucking must report the mileage on their trucks each week. The mileage reading of Ed's vehicle was 52,806 at the beginning of one week, and 53,431 at the end of the same week. What was the total number of miles driven by Ed that week?

A. $515 \ miles$

B. $525 \ miles$

C. $625 \ miles$

D. $658 \ miles$

24) What is the area of an isosceles right triangle that has one leg that measures $4 \ cm$?

A. $8 \ cm^2$

B. $36 \ cm^2$

C. $3\sqrt{2} \ cm^2$

D. $72 \ cm^2$

25) Which of the following is a factor of both $x^2 - 5x + 6$ and $x^2 - 6x + 8$?

   A. $(x - 2)$

   B. $(x + 4)$

   C. $(x + 2)$

   D. $(x - 4)$

26) $\dfrac{\begin{array}{r} 36\ hr.\ 38\ min. \\ -\ 23\ hr.\ 25\ min. \end{array}}{\rule{2cm}{0.4pt}}$

   A. $12\ hr.\ 57\ min.$

   B. $12\ hr.\ 47\ min.$

   C. $13\ hr.\ 13\ min.$

   D. $13\ hr.\ 57\ min.$

27) $\dfrac{14}{26}$ is equal to:

   A. 5.4

   B. 0.54

   C. 0.05

   D. 0.5

28) If $x + y = 10$, what is the value of $9x + 9y$?

   A. 192

   B. 104

   C. 90

   D. 48

29) What is the number of cubic feet of soil needed for a flower box 2 feet long, 10 inches wide, and 2 feet deep?

   A. $22\ cubic\ feet$

   B. $12\ cubic\ feet$

   C. $\dfrac{10}{3}\ cubic\ feet$

   D. $2\ cubic\ feet$

30) A car uses 20 gallons of gas to travel 460 miles. How many miles per gallon does the car use?

    A. 23 *miles per gallon*

    B. 32 *miles per gallon*

    C. 30 *miles per gallon*

    D. 34 *miles per gallon*

31) What is the reciprocal of $\frac{x^3}{15}$?

    A. $\frac{15}{x^3} - 1$

    B. $\frac{48}{x^3}$

    C. $\frac{15}{x^3} + 1$

    D. $\frac{15}{x^3}$

32) Karen is 9 years older than her sister Michelle, and Michelle is 4 years younger than her brother David. If the sum of their ages is 91, how old is Michelle?

    A. 21

    B. 26

    C. 28

    D. 29

33) Mario loaned Jett $1,400 at a yearly interest rate of 6%. After one year what is the interest owned on this loan?

    A. $1,260

    B. $140

    C. $84

    D. $30

34) Calculate the area of a parallelogram with a base of 3 feet and height of 3.2 feet.

    A. 2.8 square feet

    B. 4.2 square feet

    C. 5.8 square feet

    D. 9.6 square feet

35) Ellis just got hired for on-the-road sales and will travel about 2,500 miles a week during an 90-hour work week. If the time spent traveling is $\frac{5}{3}$ of his week, how many hours a week will he be on the road?

A. Ellis spends about 34 hours of his 90-hour work week on the road.

B. Ellis spends about 40 hours of his 90-hour work week on the road.

C. Ellis spends about 48 hours of his 90-hour work week on the road.

D. Ellis spends about 150 hours of his 90-hour work week on the road.

36) Given that $x = 0.5$ and $y = 5$, what is the value of $2x^2(y + 4)$?

A. 4.5

B. 8.2

C. 12.2

D. 14.2

37) What is the area of the shaded region if the diameter of the bigger circle is 14 inches and the diameter of the smaller circle is 10 inches.

A. $16\,\pi\ inch^2$

B. $24\,\pi\ inch^2$

C. $36\,\pi\ inch^2$

D. $80\,\pi\ inch^2$

38) A shirt costing $500 is discounted 25%. After a month, the shirt is discounted another 15%. Which of the following expressions can be used to find the selling price of the shirt?

A. $(500)(0.70)$

B. $(500) - 500(0.30)$

C. $(500)(0.15) - (500)(0.15)$

D. $(500)(0.75)(0.85)$

39) A tree 40 feet tall casts a shadow 18 feet long. Jack is 5 feet tall. How long is Jack's shadow?

  A. 2.25 ft

  B. 4 ft

  C. 5.25 ft

  D. 7 ft

40) In a school, the ratio of number of boys to girls is $7 : 3$. If the number of boys is 210, what is the total number of students in the school?

  A. 300

  B. 500

  C. 540

  D. 600

41) If x is 35% percent of 620, what is x?

  A. 185

  B. 217

  C. 402

  D. 720

42) How many square feet of tile is needed for a 19 $feet$ × 19 $feet$ room?

  A. 72 $square\ feet$

  B. 108 $square\ feet$

  C. 361 $square\ feet$

  D. 416 $square\ feet$

43) $(4x + 4)(x + 5) =$

  A. $4x + 8$

  B. $4x + 3x + 15$

  C. $4x^2 + 24x + 20$

  D. $4x^2 + 3$

44) If $x \blacksquare y = \sqrt{x^2 + y}$, what is the value of $4 \blacksquare 9$?

  A. $\sqrt{126}$

  B. 6

  C. 5

  D. 4

45) There are four equal tanks of water. If $\frac{2}{3}$ of a tank contains 200 liters of water, what is the capacity of the three tanks of water together?

  A. 1,200 liters

  B. 500 liters

  C. 240 liters

  D. 80 liters

46) What is the result of the expression?

$$\begin{vmatrix} 3 & 6 \\ -1 & -3 \\ -5 & -1 \end{vmatrix} + \begin{vmatrix} 2 & -1 \\ 6 & 4 \\ 1 & 3 \end{vmatrix}$$

  A. $\begin{vmatrix} 1 & -1 \\ 6 & 0 \\ 2 & 3 \end{vmatrix}$

  B. $\begin{vmatrix} 3 & 7 \\ -1 & -3 \\ -5 & -1 \end{vmatrix}$

  C. $\begin{vmatrix} 5 & 5 \\ 5 & 1 \\ -4 & 2 \end{vmatrix}$

  D. $\begin{vmatrix} 5 & -3 \\ -6 & 1 \\ -10 & -3 \end{vmatrix}$

47) The average weight of 20 girls in a class is $55\ kg$ and the average weight of 35 boys in the same class is $70\ kg$. What is the average weight of all the 55 students in that class?

  A. $60\ kg$

  B. $61.28\ kg$

  C. $64.54\ kg$

  D. $65.9\ kg$

IF YOU FINISH BEFORE TIME IS CALLED, YOU MAY CHECK YOUR WORK ON THIS TEST.

STOP

ISEE Upper Level Mathematics

Practice Test 2

2022-2023

Two Parts

Total number of questions: 84

Part 1 (Calculator): 37 questions

Part 2 (Calculator): 47 questions

Total time for two parts: 75 Minutes

163

ISEE Upper Level Practice Tests Answer Sheet

Remove (or photocopy) these answer sheets and use them to complete the practice tests.

ISEE Upper Level Practice Test 2

Quantitative Reasoning

1	Ⓐ Ⓑ Ⓒ Ⓓ		25	Ⓐ Ⓑ Ⓒ Ⓓ
2	Ⓐ Ⓑ Ⓒ Ⓓ		26	Ⓐ Ⓑ Ⓒ Ⓓ
3	Ⓐ Ⓑ Ⓒ Ⓓ		27	Ⓐ Ⓑ Ⓒ Ⓓ
4	Ⓐ Ⓑ Ⓒ Ⓓ		28	Ⓐ Ⓑ Ⓒ Ⓓ
5	Ⓐ Ⓑ Ⓒ Ⓓ		29	Ⓐ Ⓑ Ⓒ Ⓓ
6	Ⓐ Ⓑ Ⓒ Ⓓ		30	Ⓐ Ⓑ Ⓒ Ⓓ
7	Ⓐ Ⓑ Ⓒ Ⓓ		31	Ⓐ Ⓑ Ⓒ Ⓓ
8	Ⓐ Ⓑ Ⓒ Ⓓ		32	Ⓐ Ⓑ Ⓒ Ⓓ
9	Ⓐ Ⓑ Ⓒ Ⓓ		33	Ⓐ Ⓑ Ⓒ Ⓓ
10	Ⓐ Ⓑ Ⓒ Ⓓ		34	Ⓐ Ⓑ Ⓒ Ⓓ
11	Ⓐ Ⓑ Ⓒ Ⓓ		35	Ⓐ Ⓑ Ⓒ Ⓓ
12	Ⓐ Ⓑ Ⓒ Ⓓ		36	Ⓐ Ⓑ Ⓒ Ⓓ
13	Ⓐ Ⓑ Ⓒ Ⓓ		37	Ⓐ Ⓑ Ⓒ Ⓓ
14	Ⓐ Ⓑ Ⓒ Ⓓ			
15	Ⓐ Ⓑ Ⓒ Ⓓ			
16	Ⓐ Ⓑ Ⓒ Ⓓ			
17	Ⓐ Ⓑ Ⓒ Ⓓ			
18	Ⓐ Ⓑ Ⓒ Ⓓ			
19	Ⓐ Ⓑ Ⓒ Ⓓ			
20	Ⓐ Ⓑ Ⓒ Ⓓ			
21	Ⓐ Ⓑ Ⓒ Ⓓ			
22	Ⓐ Ⓑ Ⓒ Ⓓ			
23	Ⓐ Ⓑ Ⓒ Ⓓ			
24	Ⓐ Ⓑ Ⓒ Ⓓ			

Mathematics Achievement

1	Ⓐ Ⓑ Ⓒ Ⓓ		25	Ⓐ Ⓑ Ⓒ Ⓓ
2	Ⓐ Ⓑ Ⓒ Ⓓ		26	Ⓐ Ⓑ Ⓒ Ⓓ
3	Ⓐ Ⓑ Ⓒ Ⓓ		27	Ⓐ Ⓑ Ⓒ Ⓓ
4	Ⓐ Ⓑ Ⓒ Ⓓ		28	Ⓐ Ⓑ Ⓒ Ⓓ
5	Ⓐ Ⓑ Ⓒ Ⓓ		29	Ⓐ Ⓑ Ⓒ Ⓓ
6	Ⓐ Ⓑ Ⓒ Ⓓ		30	Ⓐ Ⓑ Ⓒ Ⓓ
7	Ⓐ Ⓑ Ⓒ Ⓓ		31	Ⓐ Ⓑ Ⓒ Ⓓ
8	Ⓐ Ⓑ Ⓒ Ⓓ		32	Ⓐ Ⓑ Ⓒ Ⓓ
9	Ⓐ Ⓑ Ⓒ Ⓓ		33	Ⓐ Ⓑ Ⓒ Ⓓ
10	Ⓐ Ⓑ Ⓒ Ⓓ		34	Ⓐ Ⓑ Ⓒ Ⓓ
11	Ⓐ Ⓑ Ⓒ Ⓓ		35	Ⓐ Ⓑ Ⓒ Ⓓ
12	Ⓐ Ⓑ Ⓒ Ⓓ		36	Ⓐ Ⓑ Ⓒ Ⓓ
13	Ⓐ Ⓑ Ⓒ Ⓓ		37	Ⓐ Ⓑ Ⓒ Ⓓ
14	Ⓐ Ⓑ Ⓒ Ⓓ		38	Ⓐ Ⓑ Ⓒ Ⓓ
15	Ⓐ Ⓑ Ⓒ Ⓓ		39	Ⓐ Ⓑ Ⓒ Ⓓ
16	Ⓐ Ⓑ Ⓒ Ⓓ		40	Ⓐ Ⓑ Ⓒ Ⓓ
17	Ⓐ Ⓑ Ⓒ Ⓓ		41	Ⓐ Ⓑ Ⓒ Ⓓ
18	Ⓐ Ⓑ Ⓒ Ⓓ		42	Ⓐ Ⓑ Ⓒ Ⓓ
19	Ⓐ Ⓑ Ⓒ Ⓓ		43	Ⓐ Ⓑ Ⓒ Ⓓ
20	Ⓐ Ⓑ Ⓒ Ⓓ		44	Ⓐ Ⓑ Ⓒ Ⓓ
21	Ⓐ Ⓑ Ⓒ Ⓓ		45	Ⓐ Ⓑ Ⓒ Ⓓ
22	Ⓐ Ⓑ Ⓒ Ⓓ		46	Ⓐ Ⓑ Ⓒ Ⓓ
23	Ⓐ Ⓑ Ⓒ Ⓓ		47	Ⓐ Ⓑ Ⓒ Ⓓ
24	Ⓐ Ⓑ Ⓒ Ⓓ			

ISEE Upper Level

Practice Test 2

Part 1 (Quantitative Reasoning)

37 questions

Total time for this section: 35 Minutes

You may NOT use a calculator for this test.

1) What is the prime factorization of 280?

   A. $2 \times 2 \times 5 \times 7$

   B. $2 \times 2 \times 2 \times 2 \times 5 \times 7$

   C. 2×7

   D. $2 \times 2 \times 2 \times 5 \times 7$

2) A basket contains 20 balls and the average weight of each of these balls is 26 g. The five heaviest balls have an average weight of 40 g each. If we remove the three heaviest balls from the basket, what is the average weight of the remaining balls?

   A. 10 g

   B. 21.33 g

   C. 30.78 g

   D. 35 g

3) How much greater is the value of $5x + 8$ than the value of $5x - 2$?

   A. 7

   B. 9

   C. 10

   D. 13

4) If 5 inches on a map represents an actual distance of 100 feet, then what actual distance does 16 inches on the map represent?

   A. 18 feet

   B. 100 feet

   C. 250 feet

   D. 320 feet

5) The circle graph below shows all Mr. Green's expenses for last month. If he spent $770 on his car, how much did he spend for his rent?

   A. $700

   B. $740

   C. $780

   D. $945

Mr. Green's monthly expenses

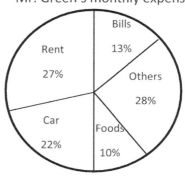

6) Alice drives from her house to work at an average speed of 52.5 miles per hour and she drives at an average speed of 60 miles per hour when she was returning home. What was her minimum speed on the round trip in miles per hour?

A. 55

B. 58.5

C. 42

D. Cannot be determined

7) The area of a circle is less than 81π. Which of the following can be the circumference of the circle?

A. $16\,\pi$

B. $18\,\pi$

C. $126\,\pi$

D. $32\,\pi$

8) Oscar purchased a new hat that was on sale for $7.38. The original price was $12.65. What percentage discount was the sale price?

A. 4.2%

B. 40.5%

C. 42%

D. 45%

9) If $f(x) = x^2 + 4$, what is the smallest possible value of $f(x)$?

A. 0

B. 4

C. 5

D. 7

10) If the sum of the positive integers from 1 to n is 2,350, and the sum of the positive integers from $n+1$ to $2n$ is 4,356, which of the following represents the sum of the positive integers from 1 to $2n$ inclusive?

A. 2,106

B. 4,356

C. 6,000

D. 6,706

11) Which of the following statements is correct, according to the graph below?

Number of Books Sold in a Bookstore

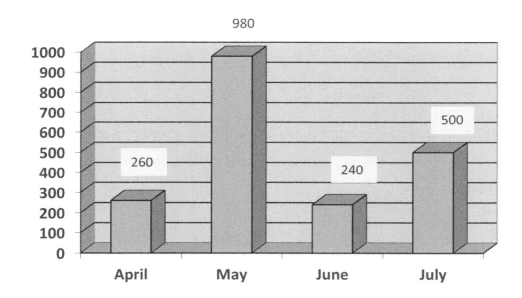

A. Number of books sold in April was twice the number of books sold in July.

B. Number of books sold in July was less than half the number of books sold in May.

C. Number of books sold in June was half the number of books sold in April.

D. Number of books sold in July was equal to the number of books sold in April and June.

12) List A consists of the numbers $\{2, 3, 8, 10, 18\}$, and list B consists of the numbers

$\{5, 6, 12, 14, 20\}$.

If the two lists are combined, what is the median of the combined list?

A. 6

B. 7

C. 8

D. 9

13) If Jim adds 120 stamps to his current stamp collection, the total number of stamps will be

equal to $\frac{5}{4}$ the current number of stamps. If Jim adds 60% more stamps to the current

collection, how many stamps will be in the collection?

A. 395

B. 550

C. 768

D. 950

14) A bag contains 18 balls: two green, five black, eight blue, a brown, a red and one white. If

11 balls are removed from the bag at random, what is the probability that a brown ball has

been removed?

A. $\frac{1}{9}$

B. $\frac{1}{6}$

C. $\frac{16}{11}$

D. $\frac{11}{18}$

15) If $x + y = 7$ and $x - y = 5$ then what is the value of $(x^2 - y^2)$?

A. 23

B. 35

C. 65

D. 90

16) What's The ratio of boys and girls in a class is $3:8$. If there are 44 students in the class, how many more boys should be enrolled to make the ratio $1:1$?

A. 8

B. 10

C. 20

D. 22

17) The area of rectangle $ABCD$ is 245 square inches. If the length of the rectangle is five times the width, what is the perimeter of rectangle $ABCD$?

A. 68 inches

B. 84 inches

C. 102 inches

D. 126 inches

18) The sum of 8 numbers is greater than 240 and less than 320. Which of the following could be the average (arithmetic mean) of the numbers?

A. 30

B. 35

C. 40

D. 45

19) Which of the following expressions gives the value of n in terms of $a, c,$ and z from the following equation?

$$a = [\frac{cz}{n}]^2$$

A. $n = ac^2z^2$

B. $n = \frac{cz}{\sqrt{a}}$

C. $n = \frac{\sqrt{a}}{cz}$

D. $n = [\frac{cz}{a}]^2$

20) Triangle ABC is similar to triangle AL

A. 4

B. 7

C. 12

D. 14

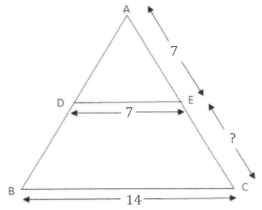

21) A gas tank can hold 20 gallons when it is $\frac{2}{5}$ full. How many gallons does it contain when it is full?

A. 125

B. 62.5

C. 50

D. 10

22)

Column A	Column B
The average of $12, 24,$ and 28	The average of $16, 20,$ and 25

A. Quantity A is greater.

B. Quantity B is greater

C. The two quantities are equal.

D. The relationship cannot be determined from the information given.

23)

Column A	Column B
$13 \times 756 \times 17$	$15 \times 756 \times 14$

A. Quantity A is greater.

B. Quantity B is greater

C. The two quantities are equal.

D. The relationship cannot be determined from the information given.

24) x is an integer

    Column A   Column B

    x $\dfrac{x}{-3}$

A. Quantity A is greater.

B. Quantity B is greater

C. The two quantities are equal.

D. The relationship cannot be determined from the information given.

25)

    Column A   Column B

The greatest value of x in $5|4x - 3| = 10$ The greatest value of x in $5|4x + 3| = 10$

A. Quantity A is greater.

B. Quantity B is greater

C. The two quantities are equal.

D. The relationship cannot be determined from the information given.

26) x is an integer

    Column A   Column B

             $(x)^2(x)^3$ $(x^2)^3$

A. Quantity A is greater.

B. Quantity B is greater

C. The two quantities are equal.

D. The relationship cannot be determined from the information given.

27) Town A is 15 kilometers due north of Town B and Town C is 8 kilometers due west of

Town B.

Column A   Column B

The shortest distance between Town C   17.5 miles

and Town A

A. Quantity A is greater.

B. Quantity B is greater

C. The two quantities are equal.

D. The relationship cannot be determined from the information given.

28)

Column A   Column B

2^2 $\sqrt[4]{81}$

A. Quantity A is greater.

B. Quantity B is greater

C. The two quantities are equal.

D. The relationship cannot be determined from the information given.

29)

Column A   Column B

6 $(33)^{\frac{1}{2}}$

A. Quantity A is greater.

B. Quantity B is greater

C. The two quantities are equal.

D. The relationship cannot be determined from the information given.

30) The selling price of a sport jacket including 18% discount is $41.

      Column A   Column B

      Original price of the sport jacket $51

A. Quantity A is greater.

B. Quantity B is greater

C. The two quantities are equal.

D. The relationship cannot be determined from the information given.

31) Jessica has to do research for her PHD. The research report she needs to read costs $10.00. however, she can copy the x pages of the report that she really needs for $0.20 per page.

      Column A   Column B

      The greatest possible value of x, if the   50

      cost of copying the x pages is less than

      the cost of purchasing the whole

      report.

A. Quantity A is greater.

B. Quantity B is greater

C. The two quantities are equal.

D. The relationship cannot be determined from the information given.

32)

      Column A   Column B

      The probability of rolling a 6 on a die   The probability of rolling an even

      and getting heads on a coin toss.   number on a die and picking a spade

                                           from a deck of 52 cards.

A. Quantity A is greater.

B. Quantity B is greater

C. The two quantities are equal.

D. The relationship cannot be determined from the information given.

33)

Column A	Column B
$(\frac{1}{4})^2$	4^{-2}

A. Quantity A is greater.

B. Quantity B is greater

C. The two quantities are equal.

D. The relationship cannot be determined from the information given.

34) Liza has a piano store, and she makes a profit of $315 on each sale of a piano and each piano costs her $1,350.

Column A	Column B
The profit expressed as a percent of the cost to Liza.	The profit expressed as a percent of the sale price.

A. Quantity A is greater.

B. Quantity B is greater

C. The two quantities are equal.

D. The relationship cannot be determined from the information given.

35) $\frac{x}{y} = \frac{3}{5}$

Column A	Column B
$\frac{x}{y}$	$\frac{x+3}{y+5}$

A. Quantity A is greater.

B. Quantity B is greater

C. The two quantities are equal.

D. The relationship cannot be determined from the information given.

36) Ina certain numbers game, x is an odd integer, and y is an even integer. An odd number is considered greater than an even number. Below are two players' results.

Column A	Column B
$(x - y)^2 + x$	$(y)(x + y)$

A. Quantity A is greater.

B. Quantity B is greater

C. The two quantities are equal.

D. The relationship cannot be determined from the information given.

37) $x^2 - 4x - 15 = 6$

Column A	Column B
x	0

A. Quantity A is greater.

B. Quantity B is greater

C. The two quantities are equal.

D. The relationship cannot be determined from the information given.

IF YOU FINISH BEFORE TIME IS CALLED, YOU MAY CHECK YOUR WORK ON THIS SECTION.

STOP

ISEE Upper Level

Practice Test 2

Part 2 (Mathematics Achievement)

- o **47 questions**

- o **Total time for this section: 40 Minutes**

- o **Calculators are not allowed at the test.**

1) $\dfrac{1}{7b^2} + \dfrac{1}{7b} = \dfrac{1}{b^2}$, then $b = ?$

A. $-\dfrac{16}{15}$

B. 6

C. $-\dfrac{15}{16}$

D. 8

2) $\dfrac{|3+x|}{7} \leq 8$, then $= ?$

A. $-38 \leq x \leq 53$

B. $-59 \leq x \leq 53$

C. $-59 \leq x \leq 38$

D. $-32 \leq x \leq 32$

3) The cost, in thousands of dollars, of producing x thousands of textbooks is

   $C(x) = x^2 + 2x$. The revenue, also in thousands of dollars, is $R(x) = 40x$. find the profit

   or loss if 10 textbooks are produced. ($profit = revenue - cost$)

A. $\$2,160\ profit$

B. $\$280\ profit$

C. $\$2,160\ loss$

D. $\$280\ loss$

4) Ella (E) is 7 years older than her friend Ava (A) who is 3 years younger than her sister Sofia

   (S). If E, A and S denote their ages, which one of the following represents the given

   information?

A. $\begin{cases} E = A + 7 \\ S = A - 3 \end{cases}$

B. $\begin{cases} E = A + 7 \\ A = S + 3 \end{cases}$

C. $\begin{cases} A = E + 7 \\ S = A - 3 \end{cases}$

D. $\begin{cases} E = A + 7 \\ A = S - 3 \end{cases}$

5) 5 less than twice a positive integer is 73. What is the integer?

A. 39

B. 41

C. 42

D. 44

6) Which of the following points lies on the line $4x + 6y = 20$?

A. $(2, 1)$

B. $(-1, 3)$

C. $(-3, 4)$

D. $(2, 2)$

7) An angle is equal to one fourth of its supplement. What is the measure of that angle?

A. 20°

B. 36°

C. 45°

D. 60°

8) 1.2 is what percent of 15?

A. 1.2

B. 8

C. 15

D. 24

9) Right triangle ABC has two legs of lengths $5\ cm$ (AB) and $12\ cm$ (AC). What is the length of the third side (BC)?

A. $4\ cm$

B. $6\ cm$

C. $8\ cm$

D. $13\ cm$

10) Simplify $8x^2y^3(2x^2y)^3 =$

A. $12x^4y^6$

B. $12x^8y^6$

C. $64x^4y^6$

D. $64x^8y^6$

11) Which is the longest time?

A. $22\ hours$

B. $1,520\ minutes$

C. $2\ days$

D. $5,200\ seconds$

12) Write 515 in expanded form, using exponents.

A. $(5 \times 10^3) + (2 \times 10^2) + (3 \times 10)$

B. $(5 \times\ 10^2) + (2 \times 10^1) - 5$

C. $(5 \times\ 10^2) + (2 \times 10^1) + 3$

D. $(5 \times 10^1) + (2 \times 10^2) + 3$

13) A company pays its writer $4 for every 400 words written. How much will a writer earn for an article with 860 words?

A. $11

B. $5.6

C. $8.6

D. $9.6

14) A circular logo is enlarged to fit the lid of a jar. The new diameter is 40% larger than the original. By what percentage has the area of the logo increased?

A. 20%

B. 30%

C. 69%

D. 96%

15) A circle has a diameter of 12 inches. What is its approximate circumference?

A. 6.28 inches

B. 25.12 inches

C. 34.85 inches

D. 37.68 inches

16) What is the area of an isosceles right triangle that has one leg that measures $8\ cm$?

A. $32\ cm^2$

B. $64\ cm^2$

C. $6\sqrt{2}\ cm^2$

D. $72\ cm^2$

17) What's the area of the non-shaded part of the following figure?

A. 192

B. 176

C. 40

D. 42

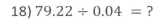

12   4

10

18

18) $79.22 \div 0.04\ = ?$

A. 19.805

B. 1,980.5

C. 1,98.05

D. 1.9805

19) A bread recipe calls for $2\frac{2}{3}$ cups of flour. If you only have $1\frac{5}{6}$ cups, how much more flour is needed?

A. 1

B. $\frac{1}{2}$

C. 2

D. $\frac{5}{6}$

20) The equation of a line is given as : $y = 5x - 3$. Which of the following points does not lie on the line?

A. $(1, 2)$

B. $(-2, -13)$

C. $(3, 12)$

D. $(2, 8)$

21) The drivers at a trucking company must report the mileage on their trucks each week. The mileage reading of Ed's vehicle was 39,750 at the beginning of one week, and 40,128 at the end of the same week. What was the total number of miles driven by Ed that week?

A. $218 \ miles$

B. $378 \ miles$

C. $410 \ miles$

D. $505 \ miles$

22) Which equation represents the statement "three plus the sum of the squares of w and x is 35"?

A. $3 + (w^2 + x) = 35$

B. $3(w^2 + x) = 35$

C. $(w^2 + x) - 3 = 35$

D. $\frac{(w^2 + x)}{3} = 35$

23) What is the solution of the following system of equations?

$$\begin{cases} -2x - y = -9 \\ -5x - 2y = 18 \end{cases}$$

A. $(-1, 2)$

B. $(-36, 81)$

C. $(36, 81)$

D. $(4, -2)$

24) What is the area of an isosceles right triangle that has one leg that measures $5\ cm$?

A. $12.5\ cm^2$

B. $25\ cm^2$

C. $6\sqrt{2}\ cm^2$

D. $72\ cm^2$

25) Which of the following is a factor of both $x^2 - 2x - 8$ and $x^2 + 6x + 8$?

A. $(x - 4)$

B. $(x + 4)$

C. $(x - 2)$

D. $(x + 2)$

26) $\dfrac{12}{25}$ is equal to:

A. 4.8

B. 0.48

C. 0.04

D. 0.4

27) If $x + y = 13$, what is the value of $8x + 8y$?

A. 192

B. 48

C. 85

D. 104

28)
$$\begin{array}{r} 37\ hr.\ 25\ min. \\ -\ 23\ hr.\ 38\ min. \\ \hline \end{array}$$

A. $12\ hr.\ 57\ min.$

B. $12\ hr.\ 47\ min.$

C. $13\ hr.\ 47\ min.$

D. $13\ hr.\ 57\ min.$

29) A car uses 18 gallons of gas to travel 450 miles. How many miles per gallon does the car get?

  A. 25 *miles per gallon*

  B. 32 *miles per gallon*

  C. 30 *miles per gallon*

  D. 34 *miles per gallon*

30) Find the perimeter of a rectangle with the dimensions 89×55.

  A. 4,895

  B. 288

  C. 144

  D. 134

31) What's the reciprocal of $\dfrac{x^3}{12}$?

  A. $\dfrac{12}{x^3} - 1$

  B. $\dfrac{48}{x^3}$

  C. $\dfrac{12}{x^3} + 1$

  D. $\dfrac{12}{x^3}$

32) Mario loaned Jett $1,300 at a yearly interest rate of 5%. After one year what is the interest owned on this loan?

  A. $1,260

  B. $120

  C. $65

  D. $30

33) Ellis just got hired for on-the-road sales and will travel about 2,900 miles a week during an 80-hour work week. If the time spent traveling is $\frac{3}{5}$ of his week, how many hours a week will he be on the road?

A. Ellis spends about 34 hours of his 80-hour work week on the road.

B. Ellis spends about 40 hours of his 80-hour work week on the road.

C. Ellis spends about 43 hours of his 80-hour work week on the road.

D. Ellis spends about 48 hours of his 80-hour work week on the road.

34) Given that $x = 0.6$ and $y = 6$, what is the value of $2x^2(y + 5)$?

A. 7.92

B. 8.2

C. 12.2

D. 13.2

35) Karen is 9 years older than her sister Michelle, and Michelle is 4 years younger than her brother David. If the sum of their ages is 85, how old is Michelle?

A. 21

B. 25

C. 29

D. 24

36) Calculate the area of a parallelogram with a base of 2 feet and height of 2.8 feet.

A. $2.8 \; square \; feet$

B. $5.2 \; square \; feet$

C. $5.6 \; square \; feet$

D. $5.0 \; square \; feet$

37) A shirt costing $200 is discounted 15%. After a month, the shirt is discounted another 15%. Which of the following expressions can be used to find the selling price of the shirt?

A. $(200)(0.70)$

B. $(200) - 200(0.30)$

C. $(200)(0.15) - (200)(0.15)$

D. $(200)(0.85)(0.85)$

38) In a school, the ratio of number of boys to girls is 3∶7. If the number of boys is 150, what is the total number of students in the school?

A. 390

B. 500

C. 540

D. 600

39) A tree 32 feet tall casts a shadow 15 feet long. Jack is 6 feet tall. How long is Jack's shadow?

A. $2.81\ ft$

B. $4\ ft$

C. $4.25\ ft$

D. $8\ ft$

40) What is the area of the shaded region if the diameter of the bigger circle is 12 inches and the diameter of the smaller circle is 6 inches.

A. $16\ \pi\ inch^2$

B. $27\ \pi\ inch^2$

C. $36\ \pi inch^2$

D. $80\ \pi inch^2$

41) What is the result of the expression?

$$\begin{vmatrix} 4 & 6 \\ -1 & -7 \\ -5 & -1 \end{vmatrix} + \begin{vmatrix} 0 & -1 \\ 6 & 0 \\ 2 & 3 \end{vmatrix}?$$

A. $\begin{vmatrix} 0 & -1 \\ 7 & 0 \\ 2 & 3 \end{vmatrix}$

B. $\begin{vmatrix} 4 & 6 \\ -1 & -3 \\ -5 & -1 \end{vmatrix}$

C. $\begin{vmatrix} 4 & 5 \\ 5 & -7 \\ -3 & 2 \end{vmatrix}$

D. $\begin{vmatrix} 0 & -3 \\ -7 & 0 \\ -10 & -3 \end{vmatrix}$

42) How many square feet of tile is needed for a 17 foot × 17 foot room?

A. $72\ square\ feet$

B. $108\ square\ feet$

C. $289\ square\ feet$

D. $216\ square\ feet$

43) $(3x + 4)\ (x + 5) =$

A. $4x + 8$

B. $3x + 3x + 20$

C. $3x^2 + 19x + 20$

D. $3x^2 + 3$

44) If $x \blacksquare y = \sqrt{x^2 + y}$, what is the value of $7 \blacksquare 15$?

A. $\sqrt{126}$

B. 8

C. 4

D. 3

45) There are three equal tanks of water. If $\frac{2}{5}$ of a tank contains 150 liters of water, what is the capacity of the three tanks of water together?

A. 1,125 liters

B. 500 liters

C. 240 liters

D. 80 liters

46) The average weight of 18 girls in a class is $50\ kg$ and the average weight of 32 boys in the same class is $62\ kg$. What is the average weight of all the 50 students in that class?

A. $50\ kg$

B. $57.68\ kg$

C. $61.68\ kg$

D. $61.9\ kg$

47) If x is 45% percent of 720, what is x?

A. 185

B. 324

C. 402

D. 720

IF YOU FINISH BEFORE TIME IS CALLED, YOU MAY CHECK YOUR WORK ON THIS TEST.

STOP

ISEE Upper Level Mathematics Practice Tests Answer Keys

Now, it's time to review your results to see where you went wrong and what areas you need to improve.

ISEE Upper Level Math Practice Test 1 Answer Key										
Quantitative Reasoning						**Mathematics Achievement**				
1	C	17	D	33	D	1	D	17	B	33	C
2	B	18	D	34	B	2	D	18	A	34	D
3	D	19	D	35	B	3	A	19	D	35	D
4	A	20	B	36	A	4	B	20	D	36	A
5	A	21	B	37	A	5	A	21	B	37	B
6	C	22	A			6	B	22	C	38	D
7	C	23	B			7	B	23	C	39	A
8	D	24	A			8	C	24	A	40	A
9	D	25	B			9	D	25	A	41	B
10	C	26	D			10	A	26	C	42	C
11	C	27	C			11	C	27	B	43	C
12	D	28	A			12	C	28	C	44	C
13	D	29	A			13	C	29	C	45	A
14	D	30	D			14	B	30	A	46	C
15	B	31	D			15	C	31	D	47	C
16	A	32	A			16	B	32	B		

ISEE Upper Level Math Practice Test 2 Answer Key

Quantitative Reasoning							Mathematics Achievement						
1	D	17	B	33	C		1	B	17	B	33	D
2	B	18	B	34	A		2	B	18	B	34	A
3	C	19	B	35	C		3	B	19	D	35	D
4	D	20	B	36	C		4	D	20	D	36	C
5	D	21	C	37	D		5	A	21	B	37	D
6	D	22	A				6	D	22	A	38	B
7	A	23	A				7	B	23	B	39	A
8	C	24	D				8	B	24	A	40	B
9	B	25	A				9	D	25	D	41	C
10	D	26	D				10	D	26	B	42	C
11	D	27	B				11	C	27	D	43	C
12	D	28	A				12	B	28	C	44	B
13	C	29	A				13	C	29	A	45	A
14	D	30	B				14	D	30	B	46	B
15	B	31	B				15	D	31	D	47	B
16	C	32	B				16	A	32	C		

ISEE Upper Level Mathematics Practice Test 1 Explanations

Quantitative Reasoning

1) Choice C is correct

$(4x + 9) - (4x - 3) = 4x - 4x + 9 + 3 = 12$

2) Choice B is correct

Find the value of each choice:

$2 \times 2 \times 5 \times 5 = 100$

$2 \times 2 \times 2 \times 5 \times 5 \times 7 = 1,400$

$2 \times 7 = 14$

$2 \times 2 \times 2 \times 5 \times 7 = 280$

3) Choice D is correct

Write a proportion and solve. $\frac{6 in}{150 feet} = \frac{20 in}{x} \rightarrow x = \frac{150 \times 20}{6} = 500 \, feet$

4) Choice A is correct

Let x be all expenses, then $\frac{22}{100}x = \$550 \ \rightarrow x = \frac{100 \times \$550}{22} = \$2,500$

He spent for his rent: $\frac{27}{100} \times \$2,500 = \$675$

5) Choice A is correct

Area of the circle is less than $14\,\pi$. Use the formula of areas of circles. $Area = \pi r^2 \Rightarrow$ $49\,\pi > \pi r^2 \Rightarrow 49 > r^2 \Rightarrow r < 7$. Radius of the circle is less than 7. Let's put 7 for the radius. Now, use the circumference formula: $Circumference = 2\pi r = 2\pi\,(7) = 14\,\pi$. Since the radius of the circle is less than 7. Then, the circumference of the circle must be less than $14\,\pi$. Only choice A is less than $14\,\pi$

6) Choice C is correct

Recall that the formula for the average is: $Average = \frac{sum\ of\ data}{number\ of\ data}$

First, compute the total weight of all balls in the basket: $35g = \frac{total\ weight}{25\ balls}$

$35g \times 25 = total\ weight = 875g$

Next, find the total weight of the 5 largest marbles: $50g = \frac{total\ weight}{5\ marbles}$

$50\ g \times 5 = total\ weight = 250\ g$

The total weight of the heaviest balls is $250\ g$. Then, the total weight of the remaining 20 balls is $625g$. $875\ g - 250\ g = 625\ g$.

The average weight of the remaining balls: $Average = \frac{625\ g}{20\ marbles} = 31.25g$ per ball

7) Choice C is correct

The smallest possible value of $f(x)$ will occur when $x = 0$. Since x^2 is always positive, any positive or negative value of x will make the value of $f(x)$ greater than 6. Substitute 0 for x and evaluate the expression: $f(0) = (0)^2 + 6 = 6$

8) Choice D is correct

There is not enough information to determine the answer of the question. An average speed represents a distance divided by time and it does not provide information about the speed at specific time. Alice could drove exactly 45 miles per hour from start to finish, or she could drive 65 miles per hour for half of distance and 45 miles per hour for the other half.

9) Choice D is correct

There are 2 sets of values, one set from 1 to n, and the other set from $n + 1$ to $2n$. Since the second set begins immediately after the first set, the two sets can be combined. The sum of the positive integers from 1 to $2n$ inclusive is equal to the sum of the positive integers from 1 to n plus the sum of the positive integers from $n + 1$ to $2n$: $3,350 + 4,866 = 8,216$

10) Choice C is correct

The percentage discount is the reduction in price divided by the original price. The difference between original price and sale price is: $\$14.65 - \$8.34 = \$6.31$

The percentage discount is this difference divided by the original price: $\$6.31 \div \$14.65 \cong 0.43$

Convert the decimal to a percentage by multiplying by 100%: $0.43 \times 100\% = 43\%$

11) Choice C is correct

Let's review the choices provided:

A. Number of books sold in April is: 480

Number of books sold in July is: $960 \rightarrow \frac{480}{960} = \frac{48}{96} = \frac{1}{2}$

B.   number of books sold in July is: 960

Half the number of books sold in May is: $\frac{1,360}{2} = 680 \rightarrow 960 > 680$

C.   number of books sold in June is: 240

Half the number of books sold in April is: $\frac{480}{2} = 240 \rightarrow 240 = 240$

D. $480 + 240 = 720 < 960$

Only choice C is correct.

12) Choice D is correct

The median of a set of data is the value located in the middle of the data set. Combine the 2 sets provided, and organize them in ascending order: $\{2, 4, 5, 7, 9, 11, 13, 15, 16, 18\}$

Since there are an even number of items in the resulting list, the median is the average of the two middle numbers. $Median = (9 + 11) \div 2 = 10$

13) Choice D is correct

If 17 balls are removed from the bag at random, there will be one ball in the bag. The probability of choosing a brown ball is 1 out of 19. Therefore, the probability of not choosing a brown ball is 17 out of 19 and the probability of having not a brown ball after removing 17 balls is the same.

14) Choice D is correct

Let x be the number of current stamps in the collection. Then: $\frac{4}{3}x - x = 150 \rightarrow \frac{1}{3}x = 150 \rightarrow x = 450$, 40% more of 450 is: $450 + 0.40 \times 450 = 450 + 180 = 630$

15) Choice B is correct

$(x^2 - y^2) = (x - y)(x + y)$, Then: $x^2 - y^2 = 7 \times 6 = 42$

16) Choice A is correct

The formula for the area of a rectangle is: $Area = Width \times Length$

It is given that $L = 3W$ and that $A = 108$. Substitute the given values into our equation and solve for W: $108 = w \times 3w \rightarrow 108 = 3w^2 \rightarrow w^2 = 36 \rightarrow w = 6$

It is given that $L = 3W$, therefore, $L = 3 \times 6 = 18$

The perimeter of a rectangle is: $2L + 2W$,Perimeter $= 2 \times 18 + 2 \times 6$, Perimeter $= 48$

17) Choice D is correct

The ratio of boy to girls is $7:4$. Therefore, there are 7 boys out of 11 students. To find the answer, first divide the total number of students by 11, then multiply the result by 7. $55 \div 11 = 5 \Rightarrow 5 \times 7 = 35$. There are 35 boys and 20 $(55 - 35)$ girls. So, 15 more girls should be enrolled to make the ratio $1:1$

18) Choice D is correct

The sum of 8 numbers is greater than 320 and less than 480. Then, the average of the 8 numbers must be greater than 40 and less than 60.

$$\frac{320}{8} < x < \frac{480}{8} \rightarrow 40 < x < 60$$

The only choice that is between 40 and 60 is 45.

19) Choice D is correct

Let x be number of gallons the tank can hold when it is full. Then: $\frac{5}{2}x = 35 \rightarrow x = \frac{2}{5} \times 35 = 14$

20) Choice B is correct

If two triangles are similar, then the ratios of corresponding sides are equal.

$\frac{AC}{AE} = \frac{BC}{DE} = \frac{20}{10} = 2$, $\frac{AC}{AE} = 2$

This ratio can be used to find the length of AC: $AC = 2 \times AE$

$AC = 2 \times 10 \rightarrow AC = 20$

The length of AE is given as 10 and we now know the length of AC is 20, therefore:

$EC = AC - AE$, $EC = 20 - 10,\quad EC = 10$

21) Choice B is correct

In order to solve for the variable b, first take square roots on both sides: $\sqrt{f} = \frac{cz}{b}$, then multiply both sides by b: $b\sqrt{f} = cz$. Now, divide both sides by $\sqrt{f}$: $b = \dfrac{cz}{\sqrt{f}}$

22) Choice A is correct

Column A: $5^2 = 25$, Column B: $\sqrt[3]{125} = 5$ (recall that $5^3 = 125$)

23) Choice B is correct

A number raised to the exponent $(\frac{1}{2})$ is the same thing as evaluating the square root of the

number. Therefore: $(52)^{\frac{1}{2}} = \sqrt{52}$

Since $\sqrt{49}$ is smaller than $\sqrt{52}$, column A ($\sqrt{49} = 7$) is smaller than $\sqrt{52}$.

24) Choice A is correct

The average is the sum of all terms divided by the number of terms. $21 + 29 + 37 = 87$,

$87 \div 3 = 29$, This is greater than 28.

25) Choice B is correct

Since both columns have 435 as a factor, we can ignore that number.

$16 \times 25 = 400$, $19 \times 22 = 418$, Column B is greater.

26) Choice D is correct

Since x is an integer and can be positive and negative, then the relationship cannot be

determined from the information given. Let's choose some values for x.

$x = 1$, then the value in column A is smaller. $-1 < \frac{1}{3}$

Let's choose a negative value for x. $x = -1$, then the value in column A is greater.

$1 > \dfrac{-1}{3} \rightarrow 1 > -\dfrac{1}{3}$

27) Choice C is correct

To raise a quantity to a negative power, invert the numerator and denominator, and then

raise the base to the indicated power. Therefore:

$(\frac{4}{1})^{-3} = (\frac{1}{4})^3$, The Columns are the same value.

28) Choice A is correct

First, simplify the inequality: $3x + 7 > x - 1 \rightarrow 3x - x > -1 - 7 \rightarrow 2x > -8 \rightarrow x > -4$

29) Choice A is correct

First, find the values of x in both columns.

Column A: $8|3x - 2| = 16 \rightarrow |3x - 2| = 2$

$3x - 2$ can be 2 or -2.

$3x - 2 = 2 \rightarrow 3x = 4 \rightarrow x = \dfrac{4}{3}$

$3x - 2 = -2 \rightarrow 3x = 0 \rightarrow x = 0$

Column B: $8|3x + 2| = 16 \rightarrow |3x + 2| = 2$

$3x + 2$ can be 2 or -2.

$3x + 2 = 2 \rightarrow 3x = 0 \rightarrow x = 0$

$3x + 2 = -2 \rightarrow 3x = -4 \rightarrow x = -\dfrac{4}{3}$

The greatest value of x in column A is $\dfrac{4}{3}$ and the greatest value of x in column B is 0.

30) Choice D is correct

Simplify both columns.

Column A: $(x)^5(x)^2 = x^7$

Column B: $(x^5)^2 = x^{10}$

Column A evaluates to x^7 and Column B evaluates to x^{10}. In the case where $x = 0$, the two columns will be equal, but if $x = 2$, the two columns will not be equal. Consequently, the relationship cannot be determined.

31) Choice D is correct

The probability that an event will occur + the probability that that event will NOT occur must equal 1. Since we don't have any numerical information about the probability, it is possible that the probability that event x occurs is 25%, 50% or any other percent. The probability that event x will not occur will always be 100% minus the probability that event x does occur. Because both columns can exhibit a range of values, the relationship cannot be determined.

32) Choice A is correct

Let x be the original price of the sport jacket. The selling price of a sport jacket including

20% discount is \$68. Then: $x - 0.20x = 68 \rightarrow 0.80x = 68 \rightarrow x = \frac{68}{0.80} = 85$

The original price of the jacket is \$85 which is greater than column B (\$80).

33) Choice D is correct

Factor the expression if possible. Begin by moving all terms to one side before factoring:

$x^2 - 2x - 20 = 15$

$x^2 - 2x - 35 = 0$

To factor this quadratic, find two numbers that multiply to -35 and sum to -2:

$(x - 7)(x + 5) = 0$

Set each expression in parentheses equal to 0 and solve: $x - 7 = 0$

$x = 7 , x + 5 = 0 , x = -5$

Quadratic equations can have TWO possible solutions. Since one of these is greater than 5 and one of them is less than 5, we cannot determine the relationship between the columns.

34) Choice B is correct

Recall that numbers between 0 and 1 when raised to power of positive integers become smaller. For example, $(0.5)^2 = 0.25$.

Then: $(0.82)^{27} > (0.82)^{28}$

35) Choice B is correct

Because of the word "and" the events described in each column must be calculated

separately and then multiplied: For column A: Probability of rolling a 4: $\frac{1}{6}$

Probability of getting heads: $\frac{1}{2}$, $\frac{1}{6} \times \frac{1}{2} = \frac{1}{12}$

For column B: Probability of an odd number: $\frac{3}{6} = \frac{1}{2}$

Probability of getting a spade: $\frac{13}{52} = \frac{1}{4}$, $\frac{1}{2} \times \frac{1}{4} = \frac{1}{8}$

Since $\frac{1}{8}$ is a larger number than $\frac{1}{12}$, Colum B is greater

36) Choice A is correct

Sum of one quarter, three nickels, and three pennies is: $\$0.25 + 3\,(\$0.05) + \$0.03 = \$0.43$

37) Choice A is correct

Let's consider the properties of odd and even integers:

$Odd +/- Odd = Even$

$Even +/- Even = Even$

$Odd +/- Even = Odd$

$Odd \times Odd = Odd$

$Even \times Even = Even$

$Odd \times Even = Even$

Now let's review the columns.

For column A: $x(x + y)$

$(odd)(odd + even)$

$(odd)(odd)$

(odd)

For Column B:

$(x - y) - y^2$

$(odd - even) - (even)^2$

$(odd) - (even)(even)$

$(odd) - (even)$

(odd)

Since an odd number is considered greater according to the problem statement, the answer is A.

ISEE Upper Level Math Practice Test 1

Mathematics Achievement

1) Choice D is correct.

Plug in each pair of numbers in the equation. The answer should be 20.

A. $(2, 1)$: $4(2) + 6(1) = 14$ No!

B. $(-1, 3)$: $4(-1) + 6(3) = 14$ No!

C. $(-2, 2)$: $4(-2) + 6(2) = 4$ No!

D. $(2, 2)$: $4(2) + 6(2) = 20$ Yes!

2) Choice D is correct

Let x be the integer. Then: $2x - 5 = 91$, Add 5 both sides: $2x = 96$, Divide both sides by 2: $x = 48$.

3) Choice A is correct

First, multiply both sides of inequality by 5. Then: $\frac{|3+x|}{5} \leq 8 \rightarrow |3 + x| \leq 40$

$-40 \leq 3 + x \leq 40 \rightarrow -40 - 3 \leq x \leq 40 - 3 \rightarrow -43 \leq x \leq 37$

4) Choice B is correct

Subtract $\frac{1}{5b}$ and $\frac{1}{b^2}$ from both sides of the equation. Then: $\frac{1}{5b^2} + \frac{1}{5b} = \frac{1}{b^2} \rightarrow \frac{1}{5b^2} - \frac{1}{b^2} = -\frac{1}{5b}$

Multiply both numerator and denominator of the fraction $\frac{1}{b^2}$ by 5. Then: $\frac{1}{5b^2} - \frac{5}{5b^2} = -\frac{1}{5b}$

Simplify the first side of the equation: $-\frac{4}{5b^2} = -\frac{1}{5b}$

Use cross multiplication method: $20b = 5b^2 \rightarrow 20 = 5b \rightarrow b = 4$

5) Choice A is correct

The sum of supplement angles is $180°$. Let x be that angle. Therefore, $x + 9x = 180°$

$10x = 180°$, divide both sides by 10: $x = 18°$

6) Choice B is correct

$x\% \ 26 = 1.3 \rightarrow \frac{x}{100} 26 = 1.3 \rightarrow x = \frac{1.3 \times 100}{26} = 5$

7) Choice B is correct

Plug in the value of $x = 20$ into both equations. Then: $C(x) = x^2 + 2x = (20)^2 + 2(20) = 400 + 40 = 440, R(x) = 40x = 40 \times 20 = 800 , 800 - 440 = 360$, So, the profit is $360.

8) Choice C is correct

$7x^3y^3(2x^3y)^3 = 7x^3y^3(8x^9y^3) = 56x^{12}y^6$

9) Choice D is correct

From choices provided, only choice D is correct. $E = \ 5 \ + A, A = S - 4$

10) Choice A is correct

Use Pythagorean Theorem: $a^2 + b^2 = c^2 \Rightarrow 4^2 + 3^2 = c^2 \Rightarrow 25 = c^2 \Rightarrow c = 5 \ cm$

11) Choice C is correct

$24 \ hours \ = \ 86,400 \ seconds \ , \ 1,520 \ minutes \ = \ 91,200 \ seconds$

$3 \ days \ = \ 72 \ hours \ = \ 259,200 \ seconds$

12) Choice C is correct

$C = 2\pi r \Rightarrow C = 2\pi \times 5 = 10\pi \Rightarrow \pi = 3.14 \rightarrow C = 10\pi = 31.4$ inches

13) Choice C is correct

Let's review the choices provided:

A. $(6 \times 10^3) + (2 \times 10^2) + (3 \times 10) = 6,000 + 200 + 30 = 6,230$

B. $(6 \ \times \ 10^2) + (2 \times 10^1) - \ 5 = 600 + 20 - 5 = 615$

C. $(6 \times 10^2) + (2 \times 10^1) + 3 = 600 + 20 + 3 = 623$

D. $(6 \times 10^1) + (2 \times 10^2) + 3 = 60 + 200 + 3 = 263$

Only choice C equals to 623.

Isosceles right triangle

14) Choice B is correct

First draw an isosceles triangle. Remember that two sides of the triangle are equal.

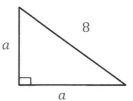

Let put a for the legs. Then: Use Pythagorean theorem to find the value of a:

$a^2 + b^2 = c^2 \rightarrow a^2 + a^2 = 8^2$

Simplify: $2a^2 = 64 \rightarrow a^2 = 32 \rightarrow a = \sqrt{32}$

$a = \sqrt{32} \Rightarrow$ area of the triangle is $= \frac{1}{2}\left(\sqrt{32} \times \sqrt{32}\right) = \frac{1}{2} \times 32 = 16 \; cm^2$

15) Choice C is correct

$\dfrac{5}{500} = \dfrac{x}{860} \Rightarrow x = \dfrac{5 \times 860}{500} = \$\, 8.6$

16) Choice B is correct

Area of a circle equals: $A = \pi r^2$, The new diameter is 20% larger than the original then the new radius is also 20% larger than the original. 20% larger than r is $1.2r$. Then, the area of larger circle is: $A = \pi r^2 = \pi(1.2r)^2 = \pi(1.44r^2) = 1.44\pi r^2$.

$1.44\pi r^2$ is 44% bigger than πr^2.

17) Choice B is correct

$89.44 \div 0.05 = 1,788.8$

18) Choice A is correct

The area of the non-shaded region is equal to the area of the bigger rectangle subtracted by the area of smaller rectangle. Area of the bigger rectangle = $14 \times 18 = 252$

Area of the smaller rectangle $= 9 \times 3 = 27$, Area of the non-shaded region = $252 - 27 = 225$

19) Choice D is correct

$2\frac{1}{2} - 1\frac{5}{4} =$, Break off 1 from 2: $2\frac{1}{2} = 1\frac{3}{2}$

$1\frac{3}{2} - 1\frac{5}{4} =$ Subtract whole numbers: $1 - 1 = 0$, Combine fractions: $\frac{3}{2} - \frac{5}{4} = \frac{1}{4}$

20) Choice D is correct

To find the maximum value of y, the expression $(x - 2)^2$ must be equal to 0. Because it has a negative sign. Since $x - 2$ is to the power of 2, it cannot be negative. To get 0 for the expression $(x - 2)^2$, x must be 2. Plug in 2 for x in the equation: $y = -(x - 2)^2 + 7 \rightarrow y = -(2 - 2)^2 + 7 = 7$, The maximum value of y is 7.

21) **Choice B is correct**

$$\begin{cases} -3x - y = -5 \\ 5x - 5y = 15 \end{cases} \Rightarrow \text{Multiplication } (-5) \text{ in first equation} \Rightarrow \begin{cases} 15 + 5y = 25 \\ 5x - 5y = 15 \end{cases}$$

Add two equations together $\Rightarrow 20x = 40 \Rightarrow x = 2$ then: $y = -1$

22) **Choice C is correct**

Let's review the choices provided. Put the values of x and y in the equation.

A. $(2, 7)$ $\Rightarrow x = 1 \Rightarrow y = 7$ This is true!

B. $(-2, -13)$ $\Rightarrow x = -2 \Rightarrow y = -13$ This is true!

C. $(4, 21)$ $\Rightarrow x = 4 \Rightarrow y = 17$ This is not true!

D. $(-4, -23)$ $\Rightarrow x = 2 - 4 \Rightarrow y = -23$ This is true!

23) **Choice C is correct**

To find total number of miles driven by Ed that week, you only need to subtract $53{,}431$ from $52{,}806$. $53{,}431 - 52{,}806 = 625 \; miles$

24) **Choice A is correct**

First draw an isosceles triangle. Remember that two sides of the triangle are equal.

Let put a for the legs. Then: Isosceles right triangle

$a = 4 \Rightarrow$ area of the triangle is $= \frac{1}{2}(4 \times 4) = \frac{16}{2} = 8 \; cm^2$

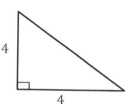

4

4

25) **Choice A is correct**

Factor each trinomial $x^2 - 5x + 6$ and $x^2 - 6x + 8$

$x^2 - 5x + 6 \Rightarrow (x - 2)(x - 3) \, , x^2 - 6x + 8 \Rightarrow (x - 2)(x - 4)$

The common factor of both expressions is $(x - 2)$.

26) **Choice C is correct**

```
   36 hr.  38 min.
 − 23 hr.  25 min.
   13 hr.  13min
```

27) **Choice B is correct**

$\frac{14}{26} = 0.538 \cong 0.54$

28) Choice C is correct

$x + y = 10$, Then: $9x + 9y = 9(x + y) = 9 \times 10 = 90$

29) Choice C is correct

First, convert all measurement to foot. One foot is 12 inches. Then: 12 inches $= \frac{10}{12} = \frac{5}{6}$ feet

The volume flower box is: length × width × height $= 2 \times \frac{5}{6} \times 2 = \frac{10}{3}$ cubic feet.

30) Choice A is correct

$\frac{460}{20} = 23$ miles per gallon

31) Choice D is correct

$\frac{x^3}{15} \quad \Rightarrow$ reciprocal is : $\frac{15}{x^3}$

32) Choice B is correct

Let's write equations based on the information provided:

$Michelle \ = \ Karen - 9$

$Michelle = David - 4$

$Karen \ + \ Michelle \ + \ David \ = \ 91$

$Karen - 9 \ = \ Michelle \Rightarrow Karen \ = \ Michelle + 9$

$Karen \ + \ Michelle \ + \ David \ = \ 91$

Now, replace the ages of Karen and David by Michelle. Then:

$Michelle + 9 \ + \ Michelle \ + \ Michelle + 4 \ = 91$

$3Michelle + 13 = 91 \Rightarrow \ 3Michelle = 91 - 13$

$3Michelle = 78$

$Michelle = 26$

33) Choice C is correct

Use interest rate formula: $Interest = principal \times rate \times time = 1{,}400 \times 0.06 \times 1 = \$84$

34) Choice D is correct

$A = bh, \qquad A = 3 \times 3.2 = 9.6$ square feet

35) Choice D is correct

Ellis travels $\frac{5}{3}$ of 90 hours. $\frac{5}{3} \times 90 = 150$, Ellis will be on the road for 150 hours.

36) Choice A is correct

Plug in the values of x and y in the expression:

$2x^2(y + 4) = 2(0.5)^2(5 + 4) = 2(0.25)(9) = 4.5$

37) Choice B is correct.

To find the area of the shaded region subtract smaller circle from bigger circle.

$S_{\text{bigger}} - S_{\text{smaller}} = \pi(r_{\text{bigger}})^2 - \pi(r_{\text{smaller}})^2 \Rightarrow S_{\text{bigger}} - S_{\text{smaller}} = \pi(7)^2 - \pi(5)^2 \Rightarrow 49\pi - 25\pi = 24\pi \; inch^2$

38) Choice D is correct

To find the discount, multiply the number by $(100\% - rate\ of\ discount)$.

Therefore, for the first discount we get: $(500)(100\% - 25\%) = (500)(0.75)$

For the next 15% discount: $(500)(0.75)(0.85)$

39) Choice A is correct

Write a proportion and solve for the missing number. $\frac{40}{18} = \frac{5}{x} \rightarrow 40x = 18 \times 5 = 90$

$40x = 90 \rightarrow x = \frac{90}{40} = 2.25\ ft$

40) Choice A is correct

The ratio of boys to girls is $7:3$. Therefore, there are 7 boys out of 10 students. To find the answer, first divide the number of boys by 7, then multiply the result by 10.

$210 \div 7 = 30 \Rightarrow 30 \times 10 = 300$

41) Choice B is correct

$\frac{35}{100} \times 620 = x \rightarrow x = 217$

42) Choice C is correct

The area of a $19\ feet\ x\ 19\ feet$ room is 361 square feet. $19 \times 19 = 361$

43) Choice C is correct

Use FOIL (First, Out, In, Last). $(4x + 4)(x + 5) = 4x^2 + 20x + 4x + 20 = 4x^2 + 24x + 20$

44) Choice C is correct

Plug in the values of x and y in the equation: $4 \blacksquare 9 = \sqrt{4^2 + 9} = \sqrt{16 + 9} = \sqrt{25} = 5$

45) Choice A is correct

Let x be the capacity of one tank. Then, $\frac{2}{3}x = 200 \rightarrow x = \frac{200 \times 3}{2} = 300$ Liters

The amount of water in four tanks is equal to: $4 \times 300 = 1{,}200$ Liters

46) Choice C is correct.

To add two matrices, first we need to find corresponding members from each matrix.

$$\begin{vmatrix} 3 & 6 \\ -1 & -3 \\ -5 & -1 \end{vmatrix} + \begin{vmatrix} 2 & -1 \\ 6 & 4 \\ 1 & 3 \end{vmatrix} = \begin{vmatrix} 5 & 5 \\ 5 & 1 \\ -4 & 2 \end{vmatrix}$$

47) Choice C is correct

$$Average = \frac{\text{sum of terms}}{\text{number of terms}}$$

The sum of the weight of all girls is: $20 \times 55 = 1{,}100 \, kg$, The sum of the weight of all boys is: $35 \times 70 = 2{,}450 \, kg$, The sum of the weight of all students is: $1{,}100 + 2{,}450 = 3{,}550 \, kg$

$$Average = \frac{3{,}550}{55} = 64.54 \, kg$$

ISEE Upper Level Mathematics Practice Test 2 Explanations

Quantitative Reasoning

1) Choice D is correct

Find the value of each choice:

$2 \times 2 \times 5 \times 7 = 140, 2 \times 2 \times 2 \times 2 \times 5 \times 7 = 560, 2 \times 7 = 14, 2 \times 2 \times 2 \times 5 \times 7 = 280$

2) Choice B is correct

Recall that the formula for the average is: $Average = \frac{sum\ of\ data}{number\ of\ data}$

First, compute the total weight of all balls in the basket:

$26\ g = \frac{total\ weight}{20\ balls}, 26g \times 20 = total\ weight = 520\ g$

Next, find the total weight of the 5 largest marbles:

$40\ g = \frac{total\ weight}{5\ marbles}, 40\ g \times 5 = total\ weight = 200\ g$

The total weight of the heaviest balls is $200\ g$. Then, the total weight of the remaining 15 balls is $320\ g. 520\ g - 200\ g = 320\ g.$

The average weight of the remaining balls: $Average = \frac{320\ g}{15\ marbles} = 21.33\ g\ per\ ball$

3) Choice C is correct

$(5x + 8) - (5x - 2) = 10$

4) Choice D is correct

First calculate the number of feet that 1 inch represents: $100\ ft \div 5\ in = 20\ \frac{ft}{in}$

Then multiply this by the total number of inches: $16\ in \times 20\ \frac{ft}{in} = 320\ ft$

5) Choice D is correct

Let x be all expenses, then $\frac{22}{100}x = \$770 \rightarrow x = \frac{100 \times \$770}{22} = \$3,500$

He spent for his rent: $\frac{27}{100} \times \$3,500 = \$945$

6) Choice D is correct

There is not enough information to determine the answer the question. An average speed represents a distance divided by time and it does not provide information about the speed at specific time. Alice could drove exactly 52.5 miles per hour from start to finish, or she could drive 60 miles per hour for half of distance and 45 miles per hour for the other half.

7) Choice A is correct

Area of the circle is less than $18\,\pi$. Use the formula of areas of circles.

$$Area = \pi r^2 \Rightarrow 81\,\pi > \pi r^2 \Rightarrow 81 > r^2 \Rightarrow r < 9$$

Radius of the circle is less than 8. Let's put 8 for the radius. Now, use the circumference formula: $Circumference = 2\pi r = 2\pi\,(9) = 18\,\pi$, Since the radius of the circle is less than 9. Then, the circumference of the circle must be less than 18π. Online choices A is less than $18\,\pi$.

8) Choice C is correct

The correct answer is (C). The percentage discount is the reduction in price divided by the original price. The difference between original price and sale price is:

$$\$12.65 - \$7.38 = \$5.27$$

The percentage discount is this difference divided by the original price:

$\$5.27 \div \$12.65 = 0.417 \cong 0.42$, Convert the decimal to a percentage by multiplying by 100%: $0.42 \times 100\% = 42\%$

9) Choice B is correct

The smallest possible value of $f(x)$ will occur when $x = 0$. Since x^2 is always positive, any positive or negative value of x will make the value of $f(x)$ greater than 4. Substitute 0 for x and evaluate the expression: $f(0) = (0)^2 + 4 = 4$

10) Choice D is correct

There are 2 sets of values, one set from 1 to n, and the other set from $n + 1$ to $2n$. Since the second set begins immediately after the first set, the two sets can be combined. The sum of the positive integers from 1 to $2n$ inclusive is equal to the sum of the positive integers from 1 to n plus the sum of the positive integers from $n + 1$ to $2n$: $2,350 + 4,356 = 6,706$

11) Choice D is correct

A. Number of books sold in April is: 260

Number of books sold in July is: $500 \rightarrow \frac{260}{500} \neq \frac{1}{2}$

B. number of books sold in July is: 500

Half the number of books sold in May is: $\frac{980}{2} = 490 \rightarrow 500 > 490$

C. number of books sold in June is: 240

Half the number of books sold in April is: $\frac{260}{2} = 130 \rightarrow 130 \neq 240$

D. $260 + 240 = 500$

Only Choice D is correct.

12) Choice D is correct

The median of a set of data is the value located in the middle of the data set. Combine the 2 sets provided, and organize them in ascending order: $\{2, 3, 5, 6, 8, 10, 12, 14, 18, 20\}$

Since there are an even number of items in the resulting list, the median is the average of the two middle numbers. Median $= (8 + 10) \div 2 = 9$

13) Choice C is correct

Let x be the number of current stamps in the collection. Then: $\frac{5}{4}x - x = 120 \rightarrow \frac{1}{4}x = 120 \rightarrow x = 480$, 60% more of 480 is: $480 + 0.60 \times 480 = 480 + 288 = 768$.

14) Choice D is correct

If 11 balls are removed from the bag at random, there will be one ball in the bag. The probability of choosing a brown ball is 1 out of 18. Therefore, the probability of not choosing a brown ball is 11 out of 18 and the probability of having not a brown ball after removing 11 balls is the same.

15) Choice B is correct

$(x^2 - y^2) = (x - y)(x + y)$, Then: $x^2 - y^2 = 7 \times 5 = 35$

16) Choice C is correct

The ratio of boy to girls is $3 : 8$. Therefore, there are 3 boys out of 11 students. To find the answer, first divide the total number of students by 11, then multiply the result by 3.

$44 \div 11 = 4 \Rightarrow 4 \times 3 = 12$, There are 12 boys and 32 $(44 - 12)$ girls. So, 20 more boys should be enrolled to make the ratio $1 : 1$

17) Choice B is correct

The formula for the area of a rectangle is: $Area = Width \times Length$

It is given that $L = 5W$ and that $A = 245$. Substitute the given values into our equation and solve for W:

$245 = W \times 5W$, $245 = 5W^2$, $W^2 = 49$, $W = 7$

It is given that $L = 5W$, therefore, $L = 5 \times 7 = 35$

The perimeter of a rectangle is: $2L + 2W$, Perimeter $= 2 \times 35 + 2 \times 7$, Perimeter $= 84$

18) Choice B is correct

The sum of 8 numbers is greater than 240 and less than 320. Then, the average of the 8 numbers must be greater than 30 and less than 40. $\frac{240}{8} < x < \frac{320}{8}$

$30 < x < 40$

The only choice that is between 30 and 40 is 35.

19) Choice B is correct

In order to solve for the variable n, first take square roots on both sides: $\sqrt{a} = \frac{cz}{n}$, then multiply both sides by n: $n\sqrt{a} = cz$, Now, divide both sides by $\sqrt{a}$:

$n = \frac{cz}{\sqrt{a}}$

20) Choice B is correct

If two triangles are similar, then the ratios of corresponding sides are equal.

$\frac{AC}{AE} = \frac{BC}{DE} = \frac{14}{7} = 2, \frac{AC}{AE} = 2$, This ratio can be used to find the length of AC:

$AC = 2 \times AE, AC = 2 \times 7, AC = 14$

The length of AE is given as 7 and we now know the length of AC is 14, therefore:

$EC = AC - AE, EC = 14 - 7, \quad EC = 7$

21) Choice C is correct

Let x be number of gallons the tank can hold when it is full. Then:

$\frac{2}{5}x = 20 \rightarrow x = \frac{5}{2} \times 20 = 50$

22) Choice A is correct

The average is the sum of all terms divided by the number of terms.

Column A $12 + 24 + 28 = 64, 64 \div 3 = 21.33$

Column B $16 + 20 + 25 = 61, 61 \div 3 = 20.33$

23) Choice A is correct

Number 756 is repeated in both columns. So, we can ignore it.

$13 \times 17 = 221, 15 \times 14 = 210$

24) Choice D is correct

Since x is an integer and can be positive and negative, then the relationship cannot be determined from the information given. Let's choose some values for x.

$x = 1$, then the value in column A is greater. $1 > \frac{1}{-3}$

Let's choose a negative value for x.

$x = -1$, then the value in column B is greater. $-1 < \frac{-1}{-3} \rightarrow -1 < \frac{1}{3}$

25) Choice A is correct

First, find the values of x in both columns.

Column A: $5|4x - 3| = 10 \rightarrow |4x - 3| = 2$

$4x - 3$ can be 2 or -2.

$4x - 3 = 2 \rightarrow 4x = 5 \rightarrow x = \frac{5}{4}$

$4x - 3 = -2 \rightarrow 4x = 1 \rightarrow x = \frac{1}{4}$

Column B: $5|4x + 3| = 10 \rightarrow |4x + 3| = 2$

$4x + 3$ can be 2 or -2.

$4x + 3 = 2 \rightarrow 4x = -1 \rightarrow x = -\frac{1}{4}$

$4x + 3 = -2 \rightarrow 4x = -5 \rightarrow x = -\frac{5}{4}$

The greatest value of x in column A is $\frac{5}{4}$ and the greatest value of x in column B is $-\frac{1}{4}$.

26) Choice D is correct

Simplify both columns.

Column A: $(x)^2(x)^3 = x^5$

Column B: $(x^2)^3 = x^6$

Column A evaluates to x^5 and Column B evaluates to x^6. In the case where $x = 0$, the two columns will be equal, but if $x = 2$, the two columns will not be equal. Consequently, the relationship cannot be determined.

27) Choice B is correct

Use Pythagorean Theorem to find the shortest distance between Town C and Town A:

$$a^2 + b^2 = c^2, \ 15^2 + 8^2 = c^2 \rightarrow 225 + 64 = c^2 \rightarrow c = 17 \ miles$$

Column B is bigger than Column A.

28) Choice A is correct

Column A: $2^2 = 4$

Column B: $\sqrt[4]{81} = 3$

29) Choice A is correct

The quantity in Column B can be simplified because fractional exponents are another way of writing roots. A number raised to the exponent (½) is the same thing as evaluating the square root of the number. Therefore: $(33)^{\frac{1}{2}} = \sqrt{33}$

Even though 33 is a prime number, and it's difficult to know the value of its square root (since it will be a decimal), we do know that 33 is between 25 and 36. The square root of 25 is 5, and the square root of 36 is 6, so the square root of 33 must be between 5 and 6. Therefore, it must be smaller than 6.

30) Choice B is correct

Let x be the original price of the sport jacket. The selling price of a sport jacket including 18% discount is \$41. Then: $x - 0.18x = 41 \rightarrow 0.82x = 41 \rightarrow x = \frac{41}{0.82} = 50$

The original price of the jacket is \$50 which is smaller than column B (\$51).

31) Choice B is correct

We need to set up the equation to maximize the value of x to determine this answer:

$0.20 \times x < 10$, $x < 10 \div 0.20$, $x < 50$

The value of x has to be less than 50, which is less than Column B.

32) Choice B is correct

Because of the word "and" the events described in each column must be calculated separately and then multiplied:

For column A:

Probability of rolling a 6: $\frac{1}{6}$

Probability of getting heads: $\frac{1}{2}$, $\frac{1}{6} \times \frac{1}{12} = \frac{1}{12}$

For column B:

Probability of an even number: $\frac{3}{6} = \frac{1}{2}$

Probability of getting a spade: $\frac{13}{52} = \frac{1}{4}$

$\frac{1}{2} \times \frac{1}{4} = \frac{1}{8}$

The correct answer is (B), since $\frac{1}{8}$ is a larger number than $\frac{1}{12}$.

33) Choice C is correct

To raise a quantity to a negative power, invert the numerator and denominator, and then raise the base to the indicated power. Therefore: $(\frac{4}{1})^{-2} = (\frac{1}{4})^{2}$

The Columns are the same value.

34) Choice A is correct

For Column A, begin by expressing the profit as a percent of the cost to Liza, where the profit is \$315 and the cost is \$1,350: $\frac{315}{1350} = 0.2333 \times 100 = 23.33\%$

For Column B, begin by calculating the sale price, which is equal to the cost plus the profit:

$\$1350 + \$315 = \$1,665$, Next, express the profit as a percent of the sale price:

$\frac{315}{1665} = 0.1891 \times 100 = 18.91\%$, Column A is greater.

35) Choice C is correct

The value of Column A is $\frac{3}{5}$ as given.

$$\frac{x}{y} = \frac{3}{5} \rightarrow 5x = 3y \rightarrow x = \frac{3}{5}y$$

Now, replace x with $\frac{3}{5}y$ in Column B. Then:

$\frac{x+3}{y+5} = \frac{\frac{3}{5}y+3}{y+5}$, Now multiply all values in both numerator and denominator by 5.

$\frac{\frac{3}{5}y+3}{y+5} = \frac{3y+15}{5y+25}$. Now, factor both numerator and denominator. Then:

$$\frac{3y + 15}{5y + 25} = \frac{3(y + 5)}{5(y + 5)} = \frac{3}{5}$$

36) Choice C is correct

Let's consider the properties of odd and even integers:

$Odd \ +/- \ Odd = Even$

$Even \ +/- \ Even = Even$

$Odd \ +/- \ Even = Odd$

$Odd \times Odd = Odd$

$Even \times Even = Even$

$Odd \times Even = Even$

If you don't have these memorized, they are easy to prove with simple numbers such as 2 and 3: $3 + 3 = 6$, $2 + 2 = 4$, $3 + 2 = 5$, $3 \times 3 = 9$, $2 \times 2 = 4$, $3 \times 2 = 6$

Now let's analyze the columns.

For column A: $(x - y)^2 - x$

$(odd + even)^2 - odd \rightarrow (odd)^2 - odd \rightarrow (odd)(odd) - odd \rightarrow odd - odd$
$$= even$$

For Column B:

$$(y)(x + y) \rightarrow (even)(odd + even) \rightarrow (even)(odd) = even$$

37) Choice D is correct

Very often, when presented with a quadratic equation, it is useful to factor it (if possible). Begin by moving all terms to one side before factoring:

$x^2 - 4x - 15 = 6$

$x^2 - 4x - 21 = 0$

To factor this quadratic, find two numbers that multiply to -21 and sum to -4:

$(x - 7)(x + 3) = 0$, Set each expression in parentheses equal to 0 and solve:

$x - 7 = 0$, $x = 7$, $x + 3 = 0$, $x = -3$

Quadratic equations can have TWO possible solutions. Since one of these is greater than 0 and one of them is less than 0, we cannot determine the relationship between the columns.

ISEE Upper Level Practice Test 2

Mathematics Achievement

1) **Choice B is correct**

Subtract $\frac{1}{7b}$ and $\frac{1}{b^2}$ from both sides of the equation. Then:

$$\frac{1}{7b^2} + \frac{1}{7b} = \frac{1}{b^2} \rightarrow \frac{1}{7b^2} - \frac{1}{b^2} = -\frac{1}{7b}$$

Multiply both numerator and denominator of the fraction $\frac{1}{b^2}$ by 7. Then:

$$\frac{1}{7b^2} - \frac{7}{7b^2} = -\frac{1}{7b}$$

Simplify the first side of the equation: $-\frac{6}{7b^2} = -\frac{1}{7b}$

Use cross multiplication method: $42b = 7b^2 \rightarrow 42 = 7b \rightarrow b = 6$

2) **Choice B is correct**

First, multiply both sides of inequality by 7. Then:$\frac{|3+x|}{7} \le 8 \rightarrow |3 + x| \le 56$

$$-56 \le 3 + x \le 56 \rightarrow -56 - 3 \le x \le 56 - 3 \rightarrow -59 \le x \le 53$$

,Choice B is correct.

3) **Choice B is correct**

Plug in the value of $x = 10$ into both equations. Then:

$$C(x) = x^2 + 2x = (10)^2 + 2(10) = 100 + 20 = \$120$$

$$R(x) = 40x = 40 \times 10 = \$400, 400 - 120 = \$280$$

4) Choice D is correct

$E = 7 + A, A = S - 3$

5) Choice A is correct

Let x be the integer. Then:$2x - 5 = 73$, Add 5 both sides: $2x = 78$, Divide both sides by 2: $x = 39$

6) Choice D is correct.

Plug in each pair of numbers in the equation. The answer should be 20.

A. $(2, 1)$: $4(2) + 6(1) = 14$ No!

B. $(-1, 3)$: $4(-1) + 6(2) = 8$ No!

C. $(-2, 2)$: $4(-2) + 6(2) = 4$ No!

D. $(2, 2)$: $4(2) + 6(2) = 20$ Yes!

7) Choice B is correct

The sum of supplement angles is 180. Let x be that angle. Therefore, $x + 4x = 180°$

$5x = 180°$, divide both sides by 5: $x = 36°$

8) Choice B is correct

$x\% \ 15 = 1.2, \dfrac{x}{100} \ 15 = 1.2 \ \rightarrow x = \dfrac{1.2 \times 100}{15} = 8$

9) Choice D is correct

Use Pythagorean Theorem: $a^2 + b^2 = c^2, 12^2 + 5^2 = c^2 \rightarrow 169 = c^2 \rightarrow c = 13 \ cm$

10) Choice D is correct

Simplify. $8x^2y^3(2x^2y)^3 = 8x^2y^3(8x^6y^3) = 64x^8y^6$

11) Choice C is correct

$22 \ hours = 79{,}200 \ seconds, 1{,}520 \ minutes = 91{,}200 \ seconds, 2 \ days =$ $48 \ hours = 172{,}800 \ seconds, 5{,}200 \ seconds$

12) Choice B is correct

Let's review the choices provided:

A. $(5 \times 10^3) + (2 \times 10^2) + (3 \times 10) = 5,000 + 200 + 30 = 5,230$

B. $(5 \times 10^2) + (2 \times 10^1) - 5 = 500 + 20 - 5 = 515$

C. $(5 \times 10^2) + (2 \times 10^1) + 3 = 500 + 20 + 3 = 523$

D. $(5 \times 10^1) + (2 \times 10^2) + 3 = 50 + 200 + 3 = 253$

Only choice B equals to 515.

13) Choice C is correct

$\frac{4}{400} = \frac{x}{860}, x = \frac{4 \times 860}{400} = \$8.6$

14) Choice D is correct

Area of a circle equals: $A = \pi r^2$

The new diameter is 40% larger than the original then the new radius is also 40% larger than the original. 40% larger than r is $1.4r$.

Then, the area of larger circle is: $A = \pi r^2 = \pi(1.4r)^2 = \pi(1.96r^2) = 1.96\pi r^2$

$1.96\pi r^2$ is 96% bigger than πr^2.

15) Choice D is correct

$C = 2\pi r, C = 2\pi \times 6 = 12\pi, \pi = 3.14 \rightarrow C = 12\pi = 37.68$ inches

16) Choice A is correct

First draw an isosceles triangle. Remember that two sides of the triangle are equal.

Isosceles right triangle

Let put a for the legs. Then:

$a = 8 \Rightarrow$ area of the triangle is $= \frac{1}{2}(8 \times 8) = \frac{64}{2} = 32\ cm^2$

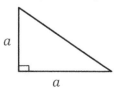

17) Choice B is correct

The area of the non-shaded region is equal to the area of the bigger rectangle subtracted by the area of smaller rectangle. Area of the bigger rectangle $= 12 \times 18 = 216$, Area of the smaller rectangle $= 10 \times 4 = 40$, Area of the non-shaded region $= 216 - 40 = 176$

18) Choice B is correct

$79.22 \div 0.04 = 1,980.5$

19) Choice D is correct

$$2\frac{2}{3} - 1\frac{5}{6} = 2\frac{4}{6} - 1\frac{5}{6} = \frac{16}{6} - \frac{11}{6} = \frac{5}{6}$$

20) Choice D is correct

Let's review the choices provided. Put the values of x and y in the equation.

A. $(1, 2)$ $\Rightarrow x = 1 \Rightarrow y = 2$ This is true!

B. $(-2, -13)$ $\Rightarrow x = -2 \Rightarrow y = -13$ This is true!

C. $(3, 12)$ $\Rightarrow x = 3 \Rightarrow y = 12$ This is true!

D. $(2, 8)$ $\Rightarrow x = 2 \Rightarrow y = 7$ This is not true!

21) Choice B is correct

To find total number of miles driven by Ed that week, you only need to subtract 39,750 from 40,128. $40,128 - 39,750 = 378$ miles

22) Choice A is correct

$3 + (w^2 + x) = 35$

23) Choice B is correct

$\begin{cases} -2x - y = -9 \\ -5x - 2y = 18 \end{cases} \Rightarrow$ Multiplication (-2) in first equation $\Rightarrow \begin{cases} 4x + 2y = 18 \\ -5x - 2y = 18 \end{cases}$

Add two equations together $\Rightarrow -x = 36 \Rightarrow x = -36$ then: $y = 81$

24) Choice A is correct

First draw an isosceles triangle. Remember that two sides of the triangle are equal.

Isosceles right triangle

Let put a for the legs. Then:

$a = 5 \Rightarrow$ area of the triangle is $= \frac{1}{2}(5 \times 5) = \frac{25}{2} = 12.5 \ cm^2$

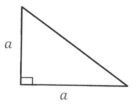

25) Choice D is correct

Factor each trinomial $x^2 - 2x - 8$ and $x^2 + 6x + 8$

$x^2 - 2x - 8 \Rightarrow (x - 4)(x + 2) \ , \ x^2 + 6x + 8 \Rightarrow (x + 2)(x + 4)$

The common factor of both expressions is $(x + 2)$.

26) Choice B is correct

$\frac{12}{25} = 0.48$

27) Choice D is correct

$x + y = 13,$ Then: $8x + 8y = 13 \times 8 = 104$

28) Choice C is correct

$$\begin{array}{r} 37 \ hr. \ \ 25 \ min. \\ - \ 23 \ hr. \ \ 38 \ min. \\ \hline 13 \ hr. \ \ 47 \ min. \end{array}$$

29) Choice A is correct

$\frac{450}{18} = 25 \ miles \ per \ gallon$

30) Choice B is correct

$Perimeter \ of \ a \ rectangle = 2(width + length) = 2(89 + 55) = 288$

31) Choice D is correct

$\frac{x^3}{12} \qquad \Rightarrow reciprocal \ is: \frac{12}{x^3}$

32) Choice C is correct

Use interest rate formula:

$Interest = principal \times rate \times time = 1,300 \times 0.05 \times 1 = \$ 65$

33) Choice D is correct

Ellis travels $\frac{3}{5}$ of 80 hours. $\frac{3}{5} \times 80 = 48$. Ellis will be on the road for 48 hours.

34) Choice A is correct

$2x^2(y + 5) = 2(0.6)^2(6 + 5) = 2\,(0.36)(11) = 7.92$

35) Choice D is correct

$Michelle = Karen - 9, Michelle = David - 4, Karen + Michelle + David = \; 85$

$Karen - 9 = Michelle \Rightarrow Karen = Michelle + 9\,, Karen + Michelle + David = 85$

Now, replace the ages of Karen and David by Michelle. Then:

$Michelle + 9 + Michelle + \; Michelle + 4 = 85,$

$3Michelle + 13 = 85 \quad \Rightarrow \; 3Michelle = 85 - 13$

$3Michelle = 72\,, Michelle = 24$

36) Choice C is correct

$A = bh, A = 2 \times 2.8 = 5.6 \; square \; feet$

37) Choice D is correct

To find the discount, multiply the number by $(100\% - rate \; of \; discount)$.

Therefore, for the first discount we get: $(200)\,(100\% - 15\%) = (200)\,(0.85)$

For the next 15% discount: $(200)\,(0.85)\,(0.85)$

38) Choice B is correct

The ratio of boys to girls is $3:7$. Therefore, there are 3 boys out of 10 students. To find the answer, first divide the number of boys by 3, then multiply the result by 10.

$$150 \div 3 = 50 \Rightarrow 50 \times 10 = 500$$

39) Choice A is correct

Write a proportion and solve for the missing number.

$$\frac{32}{15} = \frac{6}{x} \rightarrow 32x = 6 \times 15 = 90, \ 32x = 90 \rightarrow x = \frac{90}{32} = 2.8125 \cong 2.81 \ ft$$

40) Choice B is correct.

To find the area of the shaded region subtract smaller circle from bigger circle.

$$S_{bigger} - S_{smaller} = \pi \, (r \ bigger \,)^2 - \pi \, (r \ smaller \,)^2 \ \Rightarrow S_{bigger} - S_{smaller}$$
$$= \pi \, (6)^2 - \pi \, (3)^2 = 36\pi - 9\pi = 27\pi \ inch^2$$

41) Choice C is correct.

To add two matrices, first we need to find corresponding members from each matrix.

$$\begin{vmatrix} 4 & 6 \\ -1 & -7 \\ -5 & -1 \end{vmatrix} + \begin{vmatrix} 0 & -1 \\ 6 & 0 \\ 2 & 3 \end{vmatrix} = \begin{vmatrix} 4 & 5 \\ 5 & -7 \\ -3 & 2 \end{vmatrix}$$

42) Choice C is correct

The area of a $17 \ feet \times 17 \ feet$ room is 289 square feet. $17 \times 17 = 289$

43) Choice C is correct

Use FOIL (First, Out, In, Last).$(3x + 4) \, (x + 5) = 3x^2 + 15x + 4x + 20 = 3x^2 + 19x + 20$

44) Choice B is correct

Plug in the values of x and y in the equation:

$$7 \blacksquare 15 = \sqrt{7^2 + 15} = \sqrt{49 + 15} = \sqrt{64} = 8$$

45) Choice A is correct

Let x be the capacity of one tank. Then, $\frac{2}{5}x = 150 \rightarrow x = \frac{150 \times 5}{2} = 375$ Liters

The amount of water in three tanks is equal to: $3 \times 375 = 1,125$ Liters

46) Choice B is correct

$$Average = \frac{sum\ of\ terms}{number\ of\ terms}$$

The sum of the weight of all girls is: $18 \times 50 = 900\ kg$. The sum of the weight of all boys is: $32 \times 62 = 1984\ kg$, The sum of the weight of all students is: $900 + 1984 = 2884\ kg$

$$Average = \frac{2884}{50} = 57.68\ kg$$

47) Choice B is correct

$\frac{45}{100} \times 720 = x, x = 324$

... So Much More Online!

Effortless Math Online ISEE Upper Level Math Center offers a complete study program, including the following:

✓ Step-by-step instructions on how to prepare for the Upper Level Math test

✓ Numerous Upper Level Math worksheets to help you measure your math skills

✓ Complete list of Upper Level Math formulas

✓ Video lessons for Upper Level Math topics

✓ Full-length Upper Level Math practice tests

✓ And much more...

No Registration Required.

Receive the PDF version of this book or get another FREE book!

Thank you for using our Book!

Do you LOVE this book?

Then, you can get the PDF version of this book or another book absolutely FREE!

Please email us at:

info@EffortlessMath.com

for details.

Author's Final Note

I hope you enjoyed reading this book. You've made it through the book! Great job!

First of all, thank you for purchasing this study guide. I know you could have picked any number of books to help you prepare for your ISEE Upper Level Math test, but you picked this book and for that I am extremely grateful.

It took me years to write this study guide for the ISEE Upper Level Math because I wanted to prepare a comprehensive ISEE Upper Level Math study guide to help test takers make the most effective use of their valuable time while preparing for the test.

After teaching and tutoring math courses for over a decade, I've gathered my personal notes and lessons to develop this study guide. It is my greatest hope that the lessons in this book could help you prepare for your test successfully.

If you have any questions, please contact me at reza@effortlessmath.com and I will be glad to assist. Your feedback will help me to greatly improve the quality of my books in the future and make this book even better. Furthermore, I expect that I have made a few minor errors somewhere in this study guide. If you think this to be the case, please let me know so I can fix the issue as soon as possible.

If you enjoyed this book and found some benefit in reading this, I'd like to hear from you and hope that you could take a quick minute to post a review on the book's Amazon page. To leave your valuable feedback, please visit: amzn.to/3esMGlE

Or scan this QR code.

I personally go over every single review, to make sure my books really are reaching out and helping students and test takers. Please help me help ISEE Upper Level Math test takers, by leaving a review!

I wish you all the best in your future success!

Reza Nazari

Math teacher and author

Made in United States
Orlando, FL
11 October 2023